SAY IT IN
SIX

SAY IT IN
SIX

How to say
exactly what you mean
in six minutes or less.

by Ron Hoff
author of
"I Can See You Naked"

Andrews and McMeel
A Universal Press Syndicate Company
Kansas City

Library of Congress Cataloging-in-Publication Data

Hoff, Ron.
　　Say it in six : how to say exactly what you mean in six minutes or less / by Ron Hoff.
　　　　p.　cm.
　　　ISBN 0-8362-1041-7 (pbk.)
　　　1. Public speaking.　I. Title.
　　PN4121.H4575　1996
　　808.5'1—dc20　　　　　　　　　　　　　　　　95-42234
　　　　　　　　　　　　　　　　　　　　　　　　　CIP

Designed and illustrated by Barrie Maguire.

Cartoon p. 130 used with permission of Fred H. Thomas.

ATTENTION: SCHOOLS AND BUSINESSES

Andrews and McMeel books are available at quantity discounts with bulk purchase for educational, business, or sales promotional use. For information, please write to: Special Sales Department, Andrews and McMeel, 4520 Main Street, Kansas City, Missouri 64111.

CONTENTS

CHAPTER 9

How about a Role Model for Your Six-Minute Speech?
David Brinkley's Style Can Help You "Say It in Six"

CHAPTER 10

Understanding Where and When Nervousness Strikes
Now, Let's Strike Back at Nervousness
The Palm Map

PART THREE:
Special Delivery! (In Six Minutes or Less)

CHAPTER 11

"Who Goes to the Dance?"

CHAPTER 12

Sharing Secrets with the Toastmasters
Where Do You See Yourself?

You cannot win without
the ball.
—NFL color analyst

Presentation gives you
the ball. . . .
—conventional wisdom

This book tells you how
to grab the ball and
run like hell. . . .
—Ron Hoff

SAY IT IN
SIX

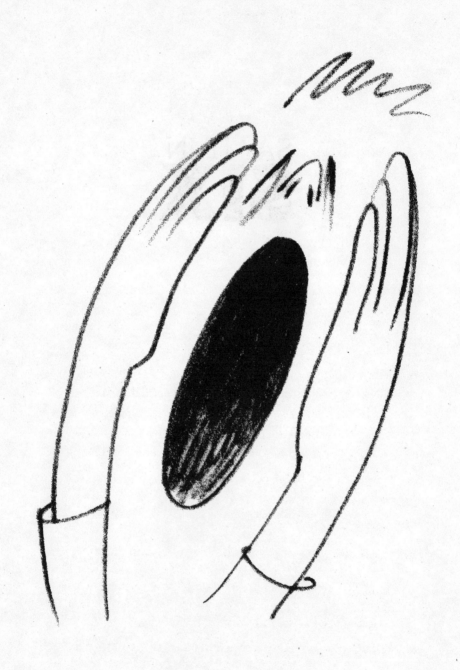

PROLOGUE

Haven't You Suffered Enough?

A Quick Quiz about You and Meetings

1. Have you ever wondered how much money your company is losing *waiting for meetings to start?*

2. Have you ever gone into a meeting and left instructions for your secretary to get you out at a certain time *whether the meeting was over or not?*

3. Have you ever forgotten what meeting you were in?

4. Have you ever endured a meeting or presentation where the speaker had at least *five* ideal places to stop—and just went on talking?

5. Have you ever been sitting in an audience and suddenly realized that you were slowly becoming engulfed in a growing roar of stomach rumbles and throat clearing?

6. Have you ever walked out of a long meeting without having the faintest idea of what you were supposed to do—or why you were invited in the first place?

7. Have you ever watched the other people in the room and noticed that their eyelids were drooping down over their pupils—and that once their eyes were completely shut, their heads would snap back to full attention and look around to see if anybody had caught them napping?

8. Have you ever been to a meeting that did nothing but make you more and more baffled about the subject being discussed? And at the end, were you so confused that you didn't dare ask a question?

9. Have you ever said to yourself, "This speaker doesn't give a hoot about me. He doesn't even know I'm here"?

10. Have you ever been sitting around a table and somebody says, "Let me tell you a little story"? You want to say, "No, no . . . not another story." But you don't—you sit there—and another turgid myth begins.

11. Have you ever sat in a meeting with a lot of people and tried to figure out how much money the company was spending— in hourly rates—just to keep all those people there?

12. Have you ever noticed that people sneak out when the film or videos begin?

How did you do? Eight "yes" answers and you've suffered enough. You're ready for *Say It in Six.*

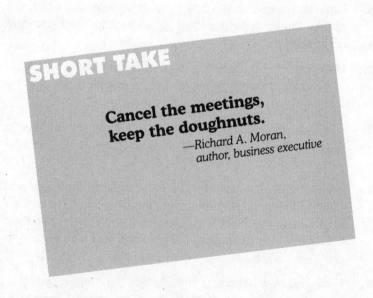

SHORT TAKE

Cancel the meetings, keep the doughnuts.
—Richard A. Moran, author, business executive

PART ONE

We Talk Too Much

BLAH! BLAH!

CHAPTER 1

You Are Looking
At **Six Minutes**

What you are reading right now is the physical mass of a six-minute speech. If you were to start with the first word of the first paragraph of this section and read aloud until you arrived at the very last word ("appreciative"), you would have talked for about six minutes.

The point being made here is crucial to the premise of this book.

In this time-driven era of the nanosecond (one-billionth of a second), six minutes is a treasure. If you know how to use it, you can make one hell of a case for yourself—or whatever you've got in mind.

Consider the case of Abe Lincoln at Gettysburg in 1863. His address on that famous battlefield has been called "the greatest short speech since the Sermon on the Mount." It took Mr. Lincoln less than three minutes to read the 269 words of his handwritten script—and that's allowing for the fact that Mr. Lincoln enjoyed words and savored them slowly.

Mr. Lincoln's fondness for brevity is well known. His second inaugural address—"With malice toward none, with charity for all"—was barely four minutes.

`01:12`

Less well known is the fact that Moses heralded the arrival of the 10 Commandments in less than five minutes.

Can you imagine how long it would take a business executive (or a politician!) to explain all 10 commandments today? He or she would have to define what a commandment is—how it differs from regular laws, such as ordinances and the like. Then, the audience would have to be told the advantages and disadvantages of each commandment. ("Do we really want to get involved in peo-

ple's sex lives . . . I mean, really?") And who's going to police these new edicts—from which budget?

I can hear this speech rumbling on for at least an hour. *Forbes* magazine says most speeches last about 40 minutes. An optimistic estimate. `01:38`

Susan B. Anthony made one of the strongest speeches for women's rights in American history—and she did it in less than five minutes. It happened in 1872, over a hundred years ago.

Five minutes! Today, it takes most people five minutes to give a speaker a proper introduction.

Remember Lou Gehrig's farewell speech to baseball?

If you're a bit young to remember that dramatic Fourth of July in 1939, you may remember the famous line that brought the house down. "Today, I consider myself the luckiest man on the face of the earth." He was dying, of course, from an incurable affliction—now known as Lou Gehrig's disease.

Sixty thousand people were in Yankee Stadium that day, many in tears. It was an unforgettable *two* minutes. Less than two years later, at age 37, he was dead.

On the very day that Nelson Mandela was released from prison in South Africa, after serving 27 years for civil disobedience, he delivered the stunning speech that marked the end of apartheid. He spoke for *five* minutes.

It has been said that Winston Churchill's oratory `03:02` saved Britain from defeat in World War II. You will find the most stirring words of his "Never Give In" speech on page 27. The entire address was six minutes long. "Blood, Sweat, and Tears" was even shorter—two and a half minutes.

Why does brevity so often accompany greatness?

- Could it be that the short speech is really the bedrock of our civilization—and, as the decades have passed, we have allowed ourselves to become more talkative while actually saying *less*?

- Could it be that our language has fattened up over the years and is now flabby and slow instead of lean and quick? I give you *paradigm, normative, redactive, suboptimal, dejobbing, countercul-*

tural, demassfication, and other words that do little more than weigh heavily on the language.

- Could it be that we lose our heads and our sense of time when we speak? Does anybody remember that 82-minute State of the Union address that prompted a 92-year-old senator to ask, "Is there going to be an intermission?"

`04:46`

- Could it be that we are so uncertain of ourselves that we burden everything with qualifiers and disclaimers? How many times have you heard the phrase, "Well, don't quote me on this, but . . ."?

- Could it be that the shrieking "talk shows" have destroyed our desire to communicate?

- Or maybe C-SPAN has simply bored our brains into numbness.

We shall consider all of these possibilities—albeit briefly.

But, right now, it's time to consider what six minutes looks like—and to read aloud the words that fit into it. If you're seated in a crowded bus, or simply don't feel like reading this section out loud, please accept the figures on faith (see stopwatch).

Here, then, is time enough for you to get some important things off your chest. And if you conclude your talk where we are ending ours, just under six minutes, your audience will undoubtedly be impressed—and grateful. In addition to being the soul of wit, brevity seems to make people appreciative.

`05:53`

SHORT TAKE

Six minutes disciplines the mind and tightens the message.

—Hugh Dunbar,
Toastmasters International
district governor, witness to
over 4,780 six-minute speeches

Let the Revolution Begin

There's only one thing about adopting the simple premise of this book—**you must be willing to start a revolution.**

You can ignite a revolution anywhere—from a PTA gathering to a political convention—but there's one important place in your life where this particular revolution could change the decision-making process for years to come.

That place is your office. The place where you spend far too much of your time.

You will be in the best possible position to spark this revolution if you're a manager in the company—or you own it. But all you *really* need to get things going is a voice in the meetings that you attend.

And that voice has to speak up and suggest something like this: "Do we really have to spend so much time in meetings? Can't we get to the point with less palaver?"

Or maybe you're so sick of the whole everlasting situation that you just blurt it out: "Look . . . why on earth does it take us so long to reach the right decision around here? Could it be that we're suffering from overinformation—that we're drowning in detail? Maybe we could speed things up if we had information that *sharpens* the issues rather than *suffocates* them?"

Be ready for some uplifted eyebrows about now. You may be cutting close to the corporate culture. Never mind. You should also have some heads nodding with you. Not committing themselves, necessarily, but warming up to your idea.

Now you strike the match and light the fuse.

"Okay . . . let's try something . . . let's try something that will work in any meeting on any subject . . . let's try something that gives us what we need to know in six minutes or less."

This is when you may hear the first rumblings of the opposing side.

"*Six minutes! Nobody around here ever said anything in less than twenty.*"

That, of course, is the problem—stated more succinctly than you'd ever heard it before. You couldn't ask for a better opening to put your proposition out in the clear.

"Look, let me take a crack at it. Next time we have a subject that needs a decision, I'll make the presentation in six minutes or less—you can clock me—and then we'll see how long it takes us to reach the right decision. You can tell me whether the idea works or not."

What you know and they have probably forgotten is this: *Of course it works.* It's worked for all of those great speakers you read about in the prologue (from Abe Lincoln to Susan B. Anthony)—and also for two national organizations (which you'll read about shortly) that limit virtually all of their speakers to six-minute presentations.

Now, the only thing you have to do is learn the rudiments of how to "say it in six." That's where this book comes in. The chapters are short (as you might expect). The illustrations are fun. The text is easy to read, but there are no silly promises, no flimflam.

"Saying it in six" is going to require more thought from you than any speech or presentation you've ever made. Brevity means short, but it can't mean shallow. That would wreck the revolution.

SHORT TAKE

You lose.

—Calvin Coolidge, when a lady at a dinner party told him that someone had bet her that she would not get more than two words out of him

A Perfect Spot to "Say It in Six"

Meetings of this kind are known mainly for their rambling arguments and eternal monologues. A well-made, six-minute speech would stand out like an exclamation point in a sea of commas.

Where Else Can You "Say It in Six"?

1. You can propose a marriage.

2. You can sell a product.

3. You can appeal a parking ticket in traffic court (see page 141).

4. You can keep an "open meeting" from running off the tracks (see page 76).

5. You can "pitch" the idea for your screenplay to a Hollywood studio.

6. You can propose a new product to your board of directors (see page 67).

7. You can apply for a new job.

8. You can "buck up" a team that needs a shot of adrenaline.

9. You can attend a General Motors stockholder meeting—state your case in no uncertain terms—and come in comfortably under the ten-minute limitation GM imposes on stockholder comments.

10. You can propose an improvement in the operation of your condominum or co-op.

11. You can compete in reviews for pending contracts or "loose accounts."

12. You can make presentations to international companies that don't speak your language. (It will save hours in translation time!)

SHORT TAKE

The worst
of all deaths
is to be
talked to death.
—Mark Twain

*I*s There Anyplace You Can't "Say It in Six"?

■　You probably won't be able to use a six-minute speech if you're the keynote speaker at a big convention. Not that it wouldn't be a refreshing change—it's just that keynote speeches are historically *long*. Fifty minutes, usually. Keynote speeches have a *bluster* that six-minute speeches are structured *not* to have.

■　If truth be told, luncheon meetings (The Lion's Club, The Rotary Club) aren't quite ready for the six-minute speech. The reason: luncheon audiences have their own rhythms of life. After a nice meal, they want to *settle in slowly* to what the speaker has to say. It's mainly a matter of digestion. They need about 25 minutes to get their metabolism back in tune with the idea of getting up and going back to the office. They allot that time to the speaker.

■　I have heard some brilliant motivational speakers who spoke from five to seven minutes. It *can* be done. But precious few *professional* motivational speakers are going to volunteer to squeeze their *intensely dramatic* speaking styles into six straight-talking minutes. No way. Especially if they're charging the audience $200 dollars per ticket.

SHORT TAKE

The thing I hate most about meetings is that I'm there.
—James Bergsman,
President,
Northwestern
Consulting Group

CHAPTER 2

The **Burning Issue:**
Linchpin of the
Six-Minute Speech

It was 9:30 on Monday morning and we were gathered, as we always were at that time, around the general manager's highly polished Chippendale conference table.

It was the executive-committee meeting, and we were halfway around the table, reporting on our various department coups, sipping coffee, gossiping, and doing a fair amount of laughing.

There were six of us, all department heads, and we enjoyed a lively collegial spirit.

As we were talking, the CEO of the agency slipped in the back door and sat down in an antique wooden chair. He made a little dismissive gesture that said, "Don't mind me."

With his arrival, the pacing of the meeting picked up. The research director continued with his report, and then the media director popped up with hers. Things were percolating more briskly now.

Suddenly, the soft, weathered voice of our CEO filled the room. "I don't mean to intrude," he said gently, "but what's the burning issue here?"

There was a noticeable pause.

"I'm serious," he said. "I'd really like to know what's *the burning issue* for this high-powered gathering."

The general manager shifted uneasily in his chair. "It's really no big deal," he said, "it's just a way for us to touch base with each other every Monday morning."

Everybody had swiveled around to face the CEO now. He rose a little wearily to his feet. The chair creaked in sympathy.

"Well," he said, "if there's no burning issue here, why don't you just have lunch together one day this week or wait until you *do* have a burning issue that will warrant all of these lofty salaries."

He opened the door and smiled back at us. "I'm sure our stockholders would appreciate it."

The door closed softly behind him.

There was a moment of silence. Then, the general manager nodded his head to no one in particular and said, "I think these meetings are over—at least until you are otherwise notified."

Ever since that Monday morning, I have never forgotten the concept of the Burning Issue.

It is, in fact, the keystone of this book and the linchpin of the six-minute speech.

If you get nothing else from your investment in this book, I hope you will remember the concept of the Burning Issue. It can save you from so many useless meetings.

Here's the rule:

> *If you don't have a Burning Issue, don't have a meeting—don't make a speech—don't make a presentation. Make a phone call or send a fax instead.*

Most meetings should never happen. They trivialize the subject by wandering off into politics and side issues that have nothing to do with most of the people sitting around the table.

The Burning Issue is what hovers just below the surface and becomes steadily worse until somebody does something about it. It may be so complex that nobody knows how to say it, but that is seldom the case. It is usually as simple as this:

> *"We have let people go. We have cut costs to the bone. But our earnings are still flat. What in the world is wrong with us?"*

Now that's a burning issue. You feel it. It's really bothering somebody. Somebody is losing sleep over it. Somebody is hurting.

When somebody has the guts to clearly state the *Burning Issue,* that's when the meeting begins.

A Burning Issue is what *drives* an important conference. Or a book, such as this one. Which brings us right up to where we want you to be. It's time to get you involved. Here's the Burning Issue of this book.

The Burning Issue of This Book

U.S. business wastes over $40 billion* on mismanaged meetings every year. We look for all kinds of ways to cut costs and overlook the most obvious one.

We talk too much.

* from a survey by Hofstra University, Department of Management, and Harrison Conference Services

Note of Thanks: To Herb Zeltner, for his help with the Burning Issue.

CHAPTER 3

Pardon Me,
but **Why Six?**

Why six? *People hate to wait!*

In 1987, I made my first effort to acquaint U.S. executives with the six-minute speech. It was not an easy sell. "Are you crazy? Nobody can say anything in six minutes," was the usual response.

Then, America discovered the computer—and all hell broke lose. Attitudes changed very fast. Clifford Wright, the author, pretty well summed it up. "Fast is smart. Slow is stodgy—people hate to wait."

Sure enough, CEOs started stomping out of meetings that didn't get to the point in the first few minutes. And time became more precious than gold.

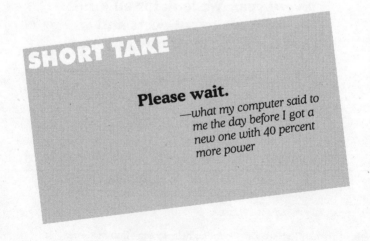

SHORT TAKE

Please wait.
—what my computer said to me the day before I got a new one with 40 percent more power

Why six? *"Not another interruption!"*

Something else happened a bit later—in the early '90s—and it really shook people up. *Reengineering* was one of its many names.

In working with CEOs and top executives around the country, I sensed something very different in the air. Every few minutes, an "emergency call" would *have to be taken* by the executive. A contract would *have to be* signed. A staffer would pop into the executive's office with "a question that simply could not wait."

Finally, I asked a CEO (and good friend) how often he was interrupted during an average day. He couldn't give me a total figure, but he gave me an answer that stuck in my head.

"With middle management virtually eliminated, I get interrupted much more than before—about every five or six minutes."

After that, the idea of packaging a presentation in six-minute segments—that is, *between interruptions*—seemed like a natural.

Why six? *The Warren Buffet factor.*

Annual meetings are driving corporate executives up the wall. Reason: Many of these well-meaning sessions have been taken over by gadflies—gabby folks with their own private agendas.

That is, until Warren E. Buffett, CEO of Berkshire Hathaway, turned things upside down by slashing the business part of his own annual meeting to six minutes.

Once the six-minute meeting was over, CEO and stockholders interacted like old chums at a high school picnic.

General Motors seems to be heading down the same road, shortening everything and clamping down tight time limits on stockholder comments.

If *speeding up* your annual meeting is on your "to do" list for next year, you might want to take a tip from Warren Buffett.

Why six? "Anchors" love it.

Six minutes has become a very valuable unit of time on TV.

—Every night, the "anchors" of the three major networks present us the day's news in less than six minutes *on camera.* Most viewers find this hard to believe. They believe the "anchors" are on for much longer. Not so. Six minutes allows the "anchor" (Jennings, Brokaw, Rather) plenty of time to "frame" the news and establish a "distinguishing personality" for his newscast.

—Six minutes (or less) works in other ways you may not suspect. *Wall Street Week* is built around the Louis Rukeyser monologue. It's his "signature" on the show. But it takes just under six minutes— and that includes his weekly report (with graphics) of the market's ups and downs.

There are dozens of other examples, but here's the point: Six minutes sounds like a short time, but it registers as a much longer period of time on your audience.

Why six? AEA endorses it.

The American Electronics Association frequently offers its members the opportunity to expose their product ideas to some of the "deepest pockets" in U.S. finance. One AEA requirement has drawn a lot of attention: "You must limit your presentation to six minutes." See page 105 for a report on a conference in Monterey, California, that features six-minute presentations.

Why six? Toastmasters toast it.

Toastmasters International sponsors 50,000 speaking contests every year. Every speaker must observe strict time limits: five to seven minutes per speech. A Toastmasters official told me that the finalists in these contests are the "best speakers in the world." I decided to see for myself (p. 113)—and pass their secrets along to you.

Why six? Even PBS uses it.

On a recent PBS network documentary entitled *Running Out of Time,* it was revealed that the average "relationship" in America (that is, one man and one woman in intimate association) has 12 minutes of talk (to each other) per day. Assuming that the two individuals get equal time (a risky assumption, to be sure), each participant in the relationship gets to talk *for a total of six minutes.*

Why six? Think of it <u>this</u> way . . .

"Oh, my . . . six minutes . . . such a short time!"
Is it? Is it really? Let's think of it another way:
—six minutes of the baby crying in the middle of the night.
—six minutes when you're waiting in line at the post office with a heavy package in your arms.
—six minutes of a terrible, terrible speech that still has another 20 minutes to go.

Why six? No time for 20!

Hey, look . . . my competition is moving into every single market I *thought* I owned. . . .
—I'm under incredible pressure to accelerate everything from making the product to closing the sale.
—The Information Highway is being built right through my business and I don't even have time to read the trade magazine I've subscribed to for the past 17 years.
—My life is a constant scramble to keep from falling behind.
—My partner has just been offered a fat salary by the company that is beating our brains out.
. . . and you want me to sit still and listen to your spiel for 20 minutes. . . .
Get real! I'll give you six minutes a week from Tuesday.

SHORT TAKE

short

KISS: Keep it s~~imple~~, stupid.

—Paul Biklen's editing of a
familiar quote. He is editor
of Let's Talk Training, a
national publication

PART TWO

Cut to the Chase

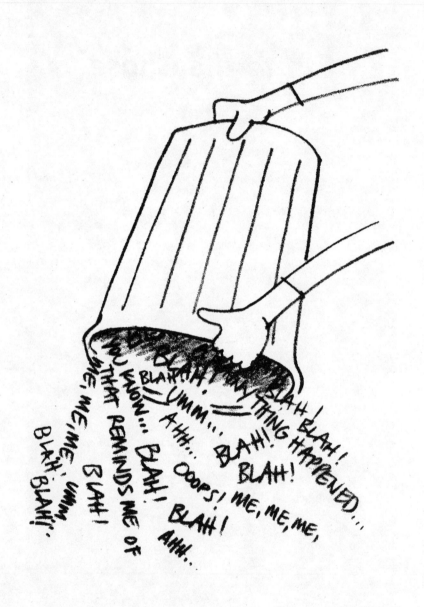

CHAPTER 4

To Slim Down to Six, We Must First
Dump the Junk!

1. **First to go: "introductory remarks."** No one has ever had the slightest idea of what this means. More likely than not, an "introductory remark" is a code phrase meaning "pure baloney." Example: "Gee, I'm so glad to be here today. It's always so good to get out of New York and see how the real people live." It's blather, pure time-wasting blather.

2. **Next up: vocalized pauses.** Vocalized pauses are used by speakers to fill the air when they don't know what to say. There are hundreds of them. "Ahhh. . . ." "Ummm. . . ." And my daughter's favorite, "and stuff like that." In many cases, the vocalized pauses are said so often that they become a part of the person's normal speech pattern. "You know" may be the number-one vocalized pause in America. It just seems to fit so naturally into almost any subject—you know? I'm not sure whether it's a promotion or a demotion to go from "you know?" to "you know what I'm saying?" This latter vocalized pause often indicates that the speaker (himself or herself) isn't exactly sure what's being said. Perfectly legitimate words sometimes get reduced to vocalized pauses. "Hopefully" is almost a vocalized pause. It is going through a stage now where it has been used so loosely—and so often—that it means almost the opposite of what it used to mean. As in, "Hopefully, we'll trim your shrubs tomorrow." I say to myself, "Oh-oh . . . they're not going to do it." Call it a virtual vocalized pause.

Whether they are gutteral sounds repeated frequently—or random obscenities—or phrases that have attached themselves to the language like fungi—all vocalized pauses can be eliminated without being missed.

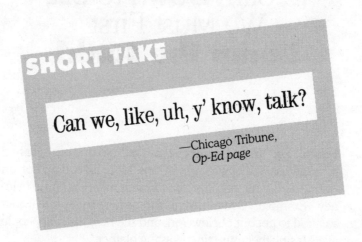

SHORT TAKE

Can we, like, uh, y' know, talk?

—Chicago Tribune,
Op-Ed page

3. **Forget about all of those nice, smooth *transitions*** that make everything flow together like oleo. "Now speaking of kinetic energy, here is Miss Energy personified. Someone who not only exudes energy in everything she does, but generates it in her colleagues." On and on. All eminently *cuttable*. This is the age of automatic connections. We don't need to be told that you have to take the elevator to get from the penthouse to the basement. The mind jumps the gaps. As George Carlin shouts when he is moving raucously from one topic to another, "Changing subjects . . . Changing subjects!"

4. This next item will make my best friends eat this page and throw the book against the wall. Can't be helped. I know my duty. **Eliminate all jokes, anecdotes, and shaggy dog stories.** For casual speeches to your local alumni association,

"stories" are ideal. With a fine bottle of wine and a box of faded old photographs, what could be better than a well-told story? For a business meeting where everybody is checking his or her watch, "stories" will get you shipped to Siberia.

5. **Next to go: those long Faulkneresque sentences.** I love Faulkner. He is an author to be read *silently*. He is not a good writer to read out loud—as in a speech. Lawyers are masters of Faulkneresque sentences. Their sentences are made of bricks. They are so loaded down with complex thoughts that they seldom make it to the brain. Have you ever listened to David Brinkley? *Really* listened to him? He uses simple language and talks in clipped cadences. He punctuates his thoughts with strategic pauses and never utters a useless word. We'll dissect the Brinkley style in a later chapter.

SHORT TAKE

Never give in.
Never give in.
Never, never, never, never—
in nothing great or small,
large or petty.
Never give in except to
convictions of honor and
good sense.
—Winston Churchill at Harrow School, England, October 29, 1941. This was part of a six-minute speech delivered to "the boys of Harrow" during World War II.

6. **"Makin' lazy circles in the sky."** Some speakers fill the room with an endless stream of words—*but they never reach a point.* The words just seem to drift leisurely, a few feet above the audience. And the poor audience sits there, barely able to contain itself, thinking, "What *is* the point of all this?" In courtrooms, you will often hear the judge say, "Just where are you going with this, counsellor?"

   Every conference or convention has two or three "lazy circles in the sky" speeches. Nobody remembers them—they are usually quite long. Even when they're reasonably brief, they *seem* interminable.

7. **"Tangent talkers" are often lured into long stretches of irrelevance.** However, they should not be confused with number six, speakers who circle endlessly and *never* connect. "Tangent talkers" are usually right-brain oriented—imaginative and funny—and when they connect, they can register unforgettably. Trouble is, you can waste a lot of time waiting for a "tangent talker" to make a point. The six-minute map on page 32 should help the "tangent talker" to stay on track and still keep the spontaneity that audiences like.

8. **Boo-boos of all kinds.** These are the time-consuming "accidents" that could have been prevented with ten minutes' worth of rehearsal. We're talking about some familiar scenes here. How many of these do you recognize?

   —The transparencies have just fallen on the floor and the speaker is on his hands and knees trying to pick them up in order. It is not a pretty sight.

   —The speaker's assistant is standing on the platform with an armload of heavy charts wondering where to put them so they will *all* be visible at the end of the talk. He is mumbling something. "I could have sworn she said there was a ledge on these walls." The walls, of course, are naked—and always have been.

   —Some damn latecomer has kicked the plug out of the wall and all of the electronic equipment is down. The speaker is literally speechless.

   —Somebody must have misunderstood the speaker, because there she is with a three-quarter-inch tape and here we are with a half-inch tape player. Tempers are getting frazzled.

There are countless other boo-boos that cause mild hysteria on the platform and tend to make members of the audience disappear in the general direction of the bar. Worse, *far* worse, time ticks away—and will never come back.

9. **Get ready for some major surgery: We want to get rid of the first half of the old-fashioned speech.** That's the half that talks about the speaker, the speaker's company, the speaker's products, the speaker's philosophy, and—on occasion—the speaker's recent book. This is the half of the speech that talks about "me, me, me" when the audience is solely concerned with itself.

10. **With the remaining portion of the speech, we'll do some David Ogilvy editing.** David, the legendary genius of advertising, was my mentor when I was a lowly copywriter at his agency. He was a *fierce* editor. He would rip whole pages from my copy, and it was always better as a result. He had another habit that took me a while to get used to. He hated adjectives and adverbs. "Nouns and verbs," he'd shout, "that's what we want." With the adjectives and adverbs gone, some sentences would just fall apart. Then, he'd cut the remains.

"See?" he'd say. "Isn't that faster?" And it always was. Most speeches could use some David Ogilvy editing.

Well, we've pretty well trashed the old-fashioned speech. Shed no tears. It was time for it to go.

SHORT TAKE

The man who makes a bad **30**-minute speech to **200** people wastes only a half hour of his own time.

But he wastes **100** hours of the audience's time—more than four days—which should be a hanging offense.

—Jenkin Lloyd Jones, *newspaper publisher*

LISTEN UP!

→

CHAPTER 5

This Is
a Six-Minute Structure
That Will Work **Forever**

If you could strip every speech before you hear it—that is, see its "bare bones" stucture—you'd know in an instant whether it was worth your time or not.

If the structure reminds you of an old clothesline, with a supporting pole on each end and lots of low points in between, you'd know you were in for a long, dreary session.

If the structure is taut, doesn't sag or bend in the middle, and has only three or four points to make—you'd probably clean off your glasses and sit a little straighter in your chair.

The side-by-side sketches on the next two pages will show you, in a very unscientific way, the difference between an old-fashioned "clothesline" structure and a faster-paced, more interesting "high wire" structure.

The "clothesline" will swing and sway for an hour. The "high wire" will crackle for no more than six minutes.

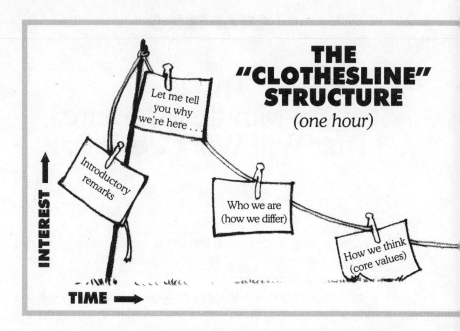

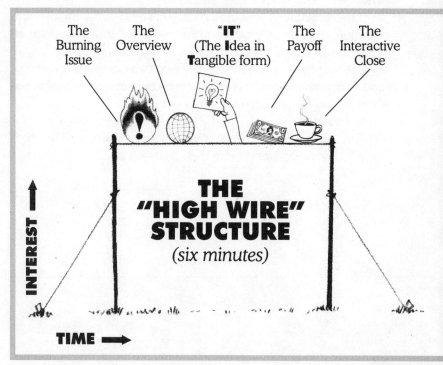

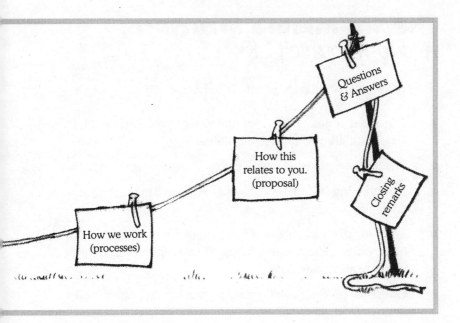

Visualize the body language at these two meetings.

The "clothesline audience" is drooping. It had high expectations at the start, but it lost interest in the middle (all those "we's" probably did it), and roused itself toward the end as the speaker asked for questions.

The "high wire" audience is hooked. Eyes stay focused. Bodies lean forward. People don't have time to get bored.

The Six-Minute Structure:
A "Do-It-Yourself" Kit

Here's what's waiting for you in "The Kit":

■ The exact times allotted for the delivery of each section. (You'll find they're surprisingly liberal.)

■ The basic elements of what's to be covered in each section.

■ How to bring "IT" to life. (That's a code word in the third section—just to keep you on your toes.)

■ Word-for-word examples of the various sections, taken from an actual six-minute speech, just to make sure everything is unmistakably clear.

■ On top of all that, you'll be doing something you've never done before—and *that's exciting!*

I. The Burning Issue: 30 seconds

You have lopped off the first half of the old fashioned "speech" and are starting where the focus has shifted from the self-interest of the speaker to the self-interest of the audience. Since you are starting where the mind of the audience is already focused, there's no need to be lengthy. (Read the following out loud.)

"We've got a great training program. We turn out terrific people. But once we've trained them in our way of doing business, the competition lures them away. They're robbing us blind. What can we do?"

That Burning Issue took 17 seconds to read aloud. You're allowed 30.

II. *The Overview: 60 seconds*

This section gives you time to say why you think the Burning Issue has developed, and where you intend to find the answer.

Read the Overview below and notice how it connects the past and present, then sets up the next section. (Remember to read it out loud.)

> *"This company believes in training its people. We believe that a training program is a part of our corporate culture—and we've had training programs for 15 years now. I did some checking, and 8 of the 12 people in this room went through our training program. That's a pretty good testimonial. But—you're right—we're losing some of our best people only months after they've completed the program. I've talked to some of them and I've noticed that attitudes are different. They've changed in recent years. Our trainees, these days, say they're building résumés. They're adding value to their worth as individuals. Once they've made themselves more valuable, they're not reluctant to cash in on that new value.*
>
> *"Frankly, loyalty doesn't mean much any more. I'm all for the training program—always have been—but I think it needs a major overhaul."*

That overview took 60 seconds to read aloud. You're allowed 60 seconds.

III. "**IT**"—The **I**dea Made **T**angible: 120 seconds

Audiences are skeptical of free-floating ideas. They've heard about "ideas" that are nothing more than a broker's notion of which stock to buy. You've got to show them that you're serious about your idea. You've got to give the audience evidence that you—or somebody—has actually done some work on it.

Your evidence must be tangible—so they can hold it in their hands, roll it around in their fingers, feel the texture, gauge the heft of it.

Maybe it's a clay model of a new product. Maybe it's an old product that has a new safety attachment. Maybe it's an architectural drawing, or a storyboard of a new production process, or a few chunks of mineral you've discovered on company property. Maybe it's a poster. Maybe it's just a proposal, but illustrated with three-dimensional art—in color!

> *"I've got a recommendation to make. I think we need to toughen up our training program. Did you know that we've never had any failures in our training program? No failures in 15 years! We've had people drop out, but not a single failure. I think we ought to toughen up our tests. It should be possible to fail, just as it is in any other legitimate training program. We should adopt a survival-of-the-fittest policy and stick to it.*

> *"We've got an eight-week program. I suggest that it be 12 weeks. I suggest that we bring in some outside consultants to toughen up our own instructors. It would do them good.*

> *"As you know, everybody who graduates from the program gets a certificate.*

> [PRESENTER HOLDS IT UP FOR ALL TO SEE.]

> *"In 15 years, it has never been updated. I asked one of our graphic arts experts to bring it into the '90s.*

[HOLDS UP THE REDESIGNED CERTIFICATE.]

"It's not only bolder and better looking, it implies that the program is tough as hell. I recommend that we make sure that everybody who has been through the program gets one of these certificates, has it framed and hung up in a place of prominence. Look how easy it is. . . .

[HE SLIDES THE REDESIGNED CERTIFICATE INTO A FRAME AND HANGS IT ON THE WALL.]

"Incidentally, I have a redesigned certificate and frame for each of the eight graduates in this room. As a final recommendation, I suggest that everybody who graduates from the "get tough" program gets a five-thousand-dollar graduation bonus—to make it harder for our competitors to steal our people. This revised program will also give our people a feeling that they have an equity here that won't be easy to replace. And, lastly, I think we'll keep more of the people we really want."

This Idea Made Tangible took two minutes to read aloud. You will be allotted the same.

IV. The Payoff: 120 seconds

This is where everybody sharpens up the pencil. This is where the famous cost/benefit ratio comes into play. The simpler you can keep this section, the better. Only the key numbers are really necessary to an experienced group of executives. But you must prove that there will be a satisfactory return on investment. No pie in the sky, please. There must be a payoff in a reasonable period of time.

If you can make the point that your "get tough" training program will produce a 80 percent retention rate (of graduates) as opposed to the current 50 percent retention rate—you will have broken the back of the Burning Issue. Maybe you establish *four years* as an acceptable period to earn back your training costs (plus bonus) on each graduate. Once you see heads nodding on these basic figures, you don't have to push it much further. Add one or two extra benefits and keep it moving.

Incidentally, coming up next is a completely buttoned-up six-minute speech with a carefully developed payoff section—so we'll be returning again to this section (the Payoff) in a few minutes.

You are allotted two minutes for the Payoff. As you'll see in the following chapters, it's more than enough time.

V. Interactive Close: 30 seconds

Here, you tell your audience members that it's their decision to make—and that you want to hear what they think about your idea.

"Now it's up to you. Before we can move ahead on the 'get tough' program, we need your approval. That, of course, will require some interaction among you. We've kept this meeting short and sweet—the way you tell us you like them—and now it's time to talk over coffee. Come on. I'll pour."

Note: Perhaps it's not appropriate for you to have an "intermission" at the end of your six-minute speech, but you can always stir up some *interaction*. Get your audience to stand up and stretch. Open a window. Maybe cold drinks are served. Here's the point: More is decided during the interaction than during a speech or presentation. Once you've delivered your six-minute speech, *break*—if only for a few seconds. Your audience must have a chance to interact before it gets down to business.

The Interactive Close will be less than 30 seconds.

SHORT TAKE

**Go, sir, gallop,
and don't forget that
the world was made
in six days.
You can ask me
for anything you like,
except time.**

—Napoleon Bonaparte, to an aide

Just to Make Certain You've Got "IT". . .
(The *I*dea made *T*angible)

"**IT**" *For Vice-President Al Gore*—A hammer and a chisel on the David Letterman show to dramatize the idea of "downsizing" the government, chipping away at bureaucratic costs. Of course, the fact that Gore wore safety goggles makes the scene even more memorable.

"**IT**" *For Ross Perot*—A series of simple charts with a pointer that had grotesque metal claws on the end. These charts, showing Perot's remedies for the economy, were the "IT" of America's first political infomercial.

"**IT**" *For Ronald Reagan*—Forty-three pounds of budget plans. Reagan slammed them down hard, saying he would never approve such a massive mess. Good. Would have been better if he'd then offered *his* budget in a nice, skinny folder.

"IT" *For a Motel Entrepreneur*—A toy caboose. The idea: a motel composed of *real* railroad cars, end to end. The Burning Issue: "We want a motel that's different, that will give people a unique experience." It's booming— near Lake Geneva, Wisconsin.

"IT" *For a Fund-Raiser*—A meal delivery service for shut-ins. The fundraiser presented a typical food basket to the audience, spreading its contents on a long table. Then, everybody in the audience got a basket. Contributions far exceeded more conventional meetings.

"IT" will be the "sound bite" in your six-minute speech— a snapshot to focus the mind.

CHAPTER 6

Time Out for a Startling Experiment— Coming to You Directly from the **White House**

It happened without much fanfare. The president of the United States made a 12-minute speech on national television.

The speech got generally favorable reviews—not great, but better than good. About a "B" from the pundits.

I heard the speech and, like most people, didn't feel strongly about it.

Then, I had an idea that bordered on blasphemy. What would happen if the 12-minute speech were cut in half? I suspected it would be better. But I wasn't positive.

When it was edited down, it almost fell into the six-minute structure we've been talking about. Please believe me. I had no political ax to grind. I just wanted to see what would happen when a good speech meets the six-minute format.

You be the judge and jury. Scan the 12-minute version. Then, take a look at the six. Which one would register more clearly in your mind?

Twelve vs. Six. It's Your Call.

On December 14, 1994, President Clinton delivered this speech. It took exactly 12 minutes.

The marginal comments are intended to be nothing more nor less than *compassionate criticism*.

My fellow Americans, ours is a great country with a lot to be proud of. But at this holiday season everybody knows that all is not well with America, that millions of Americans are hurting, frustrated, disappointed, even angry.

In this time of enormous change our challenge is both political and personal. It involves government all right, but it goes way beyond government to the very core of what matters most to us. The question is what are we going to do about it.

Slow start, Mr... President!

Let's start with the economic situation.

I ran for president to restore the American dream and to prepare the American people to compete and win in the new American economy. For too long too many Americans have worked longer for stagnant wages and less security. For two years, we pursued an economic strategy that has helped to produce over five million new jobs.

Confusing

But even though the economic statistics are moving up, most of our living standards aren't. It's almost as if some Americans are being punished for their productivity in this new economy.

We've got to change that. More jobs aren't enough, we have to raise incomes.

Fifty years ago, an American president proposed the G.I. Bill of Rights to help returning veterans from World War II go to college, buy a home,

Most of your audience wasn't born yet

and raise their children. That built this country.

Tonight, I propose a middle-class bill of rights.

There are four central ideas in this bill of rights. First, college tuition should be tax deductible. Just as we make mortgage interest tax deductible because we want people to own their own homes, we should make college tuition deductible because we want people to go to college. Specifically, I propose that all tuition for college—community college, graduate school, professional school, vocational education, or worker retraining after high school—be fully deductible, phased up to $10,000 a year for families making up to $120,000 a year.

Education, after all, has a bigger impact on earnings and job security than ever before. So let's invest the fruits of today's recovery into tomorrow's opportunity.

Second, bringing up a child is a tough job in this economy. So we should help middle-class families raise their children.

We made a good start last year by passing the Family Leave Law, making college loans more affordable and by giving 15 million American families with incomes of $25,000 a year or less an average tax cut of more than $1,000 a year.

Now, I want to cut taxes for each child under 13, phased up to $500 per child. This tax cut would be available to any family whose income is less than $75,000.

Third, we should help middle-income people save money by allowing every American family earning under $100,000 to put $2,000 a year tax-free in an I.R.A., an individual retirement account.

But I want you to be able to use the money to live on, not just retire

Good!
A handle!
Now we've started!

OK. Good!

sagging here

Too many figures!

Ah! Solid ground again.

OK! We're with you.

44

on. You'll be able to withdraw from this fund tax-free money for education, medical expenses, the purchase of a first home, the care of an elderly parent.

Fourth, since every American needs the skills necessary to prosper in the new economy, and most of you will change jobs from time to time, we should take the billions of dollars the government now spends on dozens of different training programs and give it directly to you to pay for training if you lose your job or want a better one.

one sentence!!!

We can pay for this middle-class bill of rights by continuing to reduce government spending, including subsidies to powerful interests based more on influence than need. We can sell off entire operations the government no longer needs to run and turn dozens of programs over to states and communities that know best how to solve their own problems.

Fuzzy.

My plan will save billions of dollars from the Energy Department, cut down the Transportation Department, and shrink 60 programs into 4 at the Department of Housing and Urban Development.

Much better!

Our reinventing government initiative, led by Vice President Gore, already has helped to shrink bureaucracy and free up money to pay down the deficit and invest in our people. Already we've passed budgets to reduce the federal government to its smallest size in 30 years and to cut the deficit by $700 billion.

OK, but old news.

That's over $10,000 for every American family.

In the next few days, we'll unveil more of our proposals. And I've instructed the vice president to review every single government department and program for further reductions.

OK!!!

Good—much needed!

We've worked hard to get control of this deficit after the government debt increased four times over in the 12 years before I took office. That's a big burden on you.

About 5 percent of your income tax goes to pay for welfare and foreign aid, but 28 percent of it goes to pay for interest on the debt run up between 1981 and the day I was inaugurated president.

I challenge the new Congress to work with me to enact a middle-class bill of rights without adding to the deficit and without any new cuts in Social Security or Medicare.

I know some people just want to cut the government blindly, and I know that's popular now, but I won't do it. I want a leaner, not a meaner, government that's back on the side of hardworking Americans, a new government for the new economy, creative flexible, high quality, low cost, service oriented, just like our most innovative private companies.

I'll work with the new Republican majority and my fellow Democrats in Congress to build a new American economy and to restore the American dream. It won't be easy. Believe you me, the special interests have not gone into hiding just because there was an election in November. As a matter of fact, they're up here stronger than ever. And that's why more than ever we need lobby reform, campaign finance reform, and reform to make Congress live by the laws it puts on other people.

Together we can pass welfare reform and health care reform that work.

I'll say more about what I'll do to work with the new Congress in the State of the Union address in January.

But here's what I won't do.

I won't support ideas that sound good but aren't paid for, ideas that weaken the progress we've made in the previous two years for working families, ideas that hurt poor people

More numbers, getting groggy Mr. President.

Good! Energy meter up!

Sounds familiar, sagging again!

It's a roller coaster...

who are doing their dead-level best to raise their kids and work their way into the middle class, ideas that undermine our fight against crime or for a clean environment or for better schools or for the strength and well-being of our armed forces and foreign policy.

In other words, we must be straight with the American people about the real consequences of all budgetary decisions.

My test will be: Does an idea expand middle-class incomes and opportunities? Does it promote values like family, work, responsibility, and community? Does it contribute to strengthening the new economy?

If it does, I'll be for it, no matter who proposes it.

And I hope Congress will treat my ideas the same way.

Let's worry about making progress, not taking credit.

But our work in Washington won't be enough.

And that's where you come in.

This all starts with you.

Oh, we can cut taxes and expand opportunities, but governments can't raise your children, go to school for you, give your employees who've earned it a raise or solve problems in your neighborhood that require your personal commitment.

In short, government can't exercise your citizenship. It works the other way around.

The problems of this new world are complicated, and we've all got a lot to learn. That means citizens have to listen as well as talk. We need less hot rhetoric and more open conversation, less malice and more charity. We need to put aside the politics of personal destruction and demonization that have dominated too much of our debate.

Most of us are good people trying to do better, and if we all treated each

47

other that way we would do better. We have got to be a community again.

Yes, some people do take advantage of the rest of us, by breaking the law, abusing the welfare system, and flaunting our immigration laws. That's wrong, and I'm working to stop it. But the truth is that most people in this country, without regard to their race, their religion, their income, their position on divisive issues, most Americans get up every day, go to work, obey the law, pay their taxes, and raise their kids the best they can.

And most of us share the same real challenges in this new economy.

We'll do a lot better job of meeting those challenges if we work together and find unity and strength in our diversity. We do have more in common, more uniting us than dividing us. And if we start acting like it, we can face the future with confidence. I still believe deeply that there's nothing wrong with America that can't be fixed by what's right with America.

This is not about politics as usual. As I've said for years, it's not about moving left or right, but moving forward. Not about government being bad or good, but about what kind of government will best enable us to fulfill our God-given potential. And it's not about the next election either. That's in your hands.

Meanwhile, I'm going to do what I think is right.

My rule for the next two years will be country first, and politics as usual dead last.

I hope the new Congress will follow the same rule. And I hope you will, too.

This country works best when it works together. For decades after World War II, we gave more and more Americans the chance to live

wandering.

we're off course.

OK, but too much.

ZZZZ

Good!

Good!

48

out their dreams. I know; I'm blessed to be one of them.

I was born to a widowed mother at a time when my state's income was barely half the national average. The first person in my family to finish college, thanks to money my parents couldn't really afford, scholarships, loans, and a half-a-dozen jobs.

It breaks my heart to see people with their own dreams for themselves and their children shattered, and I'm going to do all I can to turn it around. But I need your help. We can do it.

With all of our problems this is still the greatest country in the world, standing not in the twilight but at the dawn of our greatest days.

We still have a lot to be thankful for. Let's all remember that.

Happy holidays, and God bless America.

We're ending on a low note, Mr. President.

That was 12 minutes!

*T*his Is the President's 12-Minute Speech—<u>Cut in Half</u>

This version times out at six minutes. What's been lost? What's been gained? It's your call.

My fellow Americans . . . I'm not going to make any bones about it. You know it. I know it. My party took a beating in the recent midterm elections.

But I have found, as I'm sure you have found, that you can learn a lot from your losses. Moreover, you can come back stronger than ever.

That's exactly what I intend to do. And I'm not just hopeful about it. I'm absolutely convinced of it.

Tonight, you'll see some concrete results of that conviction. You'll hear some news that will be directly beneficial to you and your family. And you'll have a better understanding of what your president is planning for the immediate future.

Let's get right into that "immediate future."

Even though we have created over five million new jobs in the past two years, we need to raise incomes. Most specifically, middle-class incomes. Productivity is up, but the money in your pocket simply hasn't kept pace. We're going to start some corrective measures tonight.

There's a new program in the works—and the name is derived from a program which helped another group of Americans when they needed it. . . .

[HE SHOWS US A G.I. BILL OF RIGHTS POSTER FROM THE 1950s. IT IS UNFRAMED. HE HOLDS IT UP INFORMALLY AND SHOWS IT TO US AS HE SAYS THE FOLLOWING:]

Remember this? The G.I. Bill of Rights. It helped the returning veterans of World War II go to college, buy a home, and raise their children.

50

Tonight, I propose another bill of rights, only this one is a *Middle-Class* Bill of Rights. It's got *four* parts.

I want to tell you briefly about each part so that you get a good, clear view of the overall program.

[PAUSE]

First, college tuition should be tax deductible. It should have been done years ago—but we're going to do it now. Certainly, if we can make the interest that you pay on your mortgage tax deductible, we can help you pay for the college educations that your children deserve.

Let's be clear. I propose that tuition for *all*.college—including graduate school and worker retraining after high school—should be fully deductible, phased up to $10,000 a year for families making up to $120,000 a year.

That's the cornerstone of our Middle-Class Bill of Rights.

Second, I plan to cut taxes for each child under 13, with a $500 deduction per child. This tax cut will be available to any family making less than $75,000 per year.

Third, I plan to allow every family earning under $100,000 a year to put $2,000 a year tax-free into an Individual Retirement Account—commonly known as an IRA. You'll be able to save this money for retirement, of course, but you'll also be able to use it for any cause that's really important to you—from the purchase of a first home to the care of an elderly parent.

Fourth, I plan to reallocate billions of dollars that the government now spends on training programs and channel that money directly back to you—for you to pay for the special training that will do you the most good. This is a decision you should make, not some government bureau in Washington.

Let me see if I can put those important points into even sharper focus for you. . . .

[HE TICKS OFF EACH POINT ON HIS FINGERS AS HE LOOKS DIRECTLY INTO THE CAMERA]

—College tuition, tax deductible. That should be a big help if you've got children approaching college age.

—For each child under 13, a $500 tax deduction. That's a needed break for families with younger children.

—Two thousand dollars *tax-free*. That's how much you can put into your IRA every year and then use it as the need arises. That's just got to be good deal for *everybody*.

—Billions of dollars, formerly controlled by Washington, will now go directly to your area for your special training needs. Local control of federal funds—that's what you said you wanted. Well . . . I'm listening.

[PAUSE]

Now, the question you're asking . . . *where will the money for the Middle-Class Bill of Rights come from?*

Basically, it will come from large reductions in the Energy Department, the Transportation Department, and the Department of Housing and Urban Development.

We'll continue to reinvent the government, an initiative led by Vice President Gore. It has already helped to shrink the bureaucracy and reduce the national deficit.

Consider these key figures. . . .

We have passed budgets to reduce the federal government to its smallest size in 30 years—and to cut the deficit by $700 billion. That's over $10,000 for every American family.

You'll hear more of our proposals in the next few days. Every detail will be spelled out—every figure will have a source. But, before we get into all of those important numbers, I wanted you to have the program clearly in mind.

There's one more point I should make.

Some people in Washington just want to cut government blindly. That's not going to happen during my presidency. I want a leaner government, not a meaner government.

I'll work with Republicans and Democrats all day and all night if necessary—to put this Middle-Class Bill of Rights into place. It won't be easy. I'll need your help.

But I've found that good works never come without hard labor. To achieve mightily takes a lot of patience—and the best efforts of all concerned.

As your president, I will champion your rights in every way I can. Tonight's Middle-Class Bill of Rights is intended to enlarge your economic rights. We'll be talking about other important rights for you and your family in the very near future.

Good night, happy holidays . . . and God bless America!

SHORT TAKE

Know what's wrong with most presentations? They ought to start about halfway through.

—Tom Theobold,
banking executive

CHAPTER 7

Sharpen Your Pencil, We're Going to "Say It in Six"— **Step by Step**

*W*oodrow Wilson was asked how long *it took him to prepare a 10-minute speech.*
"Two weeks," he said.
"How long to prepare a one-hour speech?"
"One week."
"How long for a two-hour speech?"
"I'm ready now."

President Wilson says it takes a lot more time to prepare a 10-minute speech than a two-hour speech. In fact, he says, he's ready "now" for the two-hour talk.

Is he being funny?

Maybe—but there's probably more truth than humor in what he's saying.

Sounds like he might be saying this:

"I can talk off the top of my head for as long as you please—two hours, whatever. I don't need any preparation for a talk that's little more than stream of consciousness. Just let me know when you want me to stop."

A one-hour speech, he says, is something else. That's going to take some time. He'll have to get his thoughts into some kind of order. He'll have to do some sifting and sorting. He'll have to make sure his message builds to a rousing climax—and that will require some preparation time. A week, he says.

Then, for a ten-minute speech—"Let's see," he might say, "a speech that length must be important. I'll have to really crystallize my thoughts for that one. Better get my staff involved right away. Every word must be *brilliant*. Every line must be *a winner*. We'll be lucky to have that one done right in two weeks."

The shortest takes the most time.

The longest takes the least.

The six-minute process (which you're about to experience) follows Woodrow Wilson's realization that a very good short speech can only come from a merciless chopping away at a much, much longer speech. But first you talk off the top of your head—and put it all down—so that you can select the thoughts that will register with the greatest impact.

We have tried to set up this process for you so that you can understand it, and do it, as easily as possible. But we haven't strayed far from President Wilson's original wisdom.

Turn the page to begin.

"SAY IT IN SIX" STEP-BY-STEP WORKSHEET

1 *"Let's get right to the point. There's a **burning issue** here that we need to discuss."* _____

_____

_____

_____

_____

_____

_____

2 *"Here's a quick **overview**—just a bit of background."*

_____

_____

_____

_____

3 *"This led to an **idea**. . . ."* _____

_____

_____

_____

_____

_____

_____

_____

_____

_____

_____

4 *"The idea will more than pay for itself. Here's the* **payoff**. . . ."_____

_____

_____

_____

_____

_____

5 *"Here's* **what we need** *from you to get going. . . ."*

_____

_____

_____

_____

_____

_____

Some Quick Tips about That Worksheet

1. Basically, that worksheet you just saw is all you need to get started. Focus on a presentation you'll be doing soon. Then ask yourself, "What's the core of this thing? What is everybody concerned about?" When you answer those questions, you'll have the Burning Issue. Write it down fast and simple. Don't fuss with the words. Just let your brain tell you the truth.

2. Give us two or three lines of Overview. Background. Just the high spots, so your audience is with you.

3. Then, the Idea in Tangible form ("IT"). Look at page 36 if your memory needs refreshing. Write your idea in its purest possible form and show us something visual we won't forget.

4. Don't do a lot of research to find supporting data for your Payoff. Just an estimate will do for now. You can nail everything down when you're in a fact-finding mood.

5. Make sure your audience knows where you stand on the Burning Issue and ask for their reactions to your idea. Tell them you'd like a decision as soon as possible. A little coffee won't hurt about now. . . .

(Extra worksheets can be found at the back of the book.)

After the Worksheet, It's Time to "Toughen Up" Your Message. Here's How.

■ **You've got your "bare bones"—now you need to add some muscle.** Call on some of your digital information sources. Ask for assistance on the Internet or your on-line service. Get your Hi-liters going on everything you read. Run single pages of terrific text through your copier. Tack provocative clippings and relevant quotes to your cork wall. Fill up your computer files with meaty notes. Check your local video store. Spend an hour at a local bookstore. Call a columnist at your local newspaper who's written a column about your subject—or something close to it. Gather at least 10 times more data than you'll actually use.

■ **Now, work your new material into your original outline.** Don't worry about length. Worry about strength. This is where your script begins to show its mettle. It may get up off the page and march around the room. If you've got great material, use it all. Just make sure you have it placed correctly within the structure. Now, make a copy of the *new* script and read it. As you do,

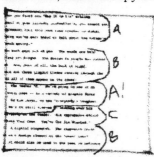

get your Magic Marker going—marking blocks of copy A, B, or C. "A" is "solid gold"—information that seems heaven-sent (like the "hanging offense" quote on page 29). "B" is "interesting and usable." Maybe it sparks a thought that you can carry further. "C" is "marginal"—interesting, possible, certainly no disgrace.

■ **This is where you invite your "relentless inner editor" to join you.** You've got some constructive cutting to do, and you should try to step outside of your usual happy-go-lucky self and be merciless. First, ask yourself if any big blocks of copy are expendable. Start with the C's. Reread chapter 4 for "easy edits." If there are any paragraphs that talk  only to your self-interest, kill them instantly. Shorten up your sentences. You don't have to have a subject and predicate in every sentence. Forget grammar—and watch the words melt away. If you have to argue with your "relentless inner editor"—let the editor win, every time. Your speech will be infinitely better.

■ **Congratulations! You've got a draft that's built like a steam engine.** Read it aloud—making small but important edits to conform to the way you talk. If anything sounds awkward to you as you say it, cut the words that trip you up. Or get rid of the cumbersome sentence. Put a stopwatch  on your next read-through. Chances are, you're very close to six minutes. If you're way over, cut a paragraph or two—not words and phrases. If you're a little over, leave it for now. If you're *under* six minutes, you might want to think about becoming an editor. But don't do anything until you read the URGENT box on the next page.

URGENT! READ THIS—

Do not, under any circumstances, get the impression that you are going to **memorize** your first six-minute speech. What we've been trying to do here is simply get the words in your head—so that you don't have to reach for them.

Memorizing is the pits. It instills the fear of forgetting. A memorized speech becomes a "performance"—a "set piece" which can be given to anybody. Audiences hate that. Every audience thinks of itself as different, unique, deserving of special treatment. You **should** memorize the structure. You can even memorize certain words and phrases that you know will work for you. **But memorizing the whole thing, word for word, imprisons your thoughts rather than setting them free.**

SHORT TAKES

When in doubt, cut it out.

—Anonymous

Paring down, paring down,
Until you reach the truth.

—Robert Haas,
Poet Laureate

What You Should Know about Time and Talk

Most people talk approx. . . . . **120** wpm
(words per minute)

News announcers talk approx. . . . . **190** wpm
(often faster)

A six-minute speaker should talk
approx. . . . . **150** wpm

At 150 wpm, a double-spaced page
of talk (with regular margins)
will take approx. . . . . **1.5** minutes when
spoken

So, you can figure a six-minute speech
is approx. . . . . **4** double-spaced pages

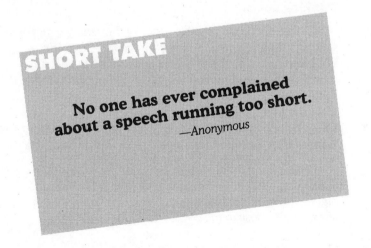

SHORT TAKE

No one has ever complained about a speech running too short.
—Anonymous

*L*et's Take a Quick Gut Check

■ **Are the people in your audience going to like this
shorter, sharper version of you—or are they going to
sit there and wonder what hit them?**

— *If you have always been a lengthy speaker, and you
suddenly sit down after six minutes, your listeners are
going to be startled, to say the least. If you think this reaction is more than they can handle—or more than you
want to subject them to—you can say something like this
right at the start. "Today, I've put myself into your shoes
and I'm going to tell you what you need to know in six
minutes." Or, you can cushion their reaction at the end by
saying, "I know how busy everybody has been and I was
determined to save your time today—so I made up my
mind to cover this subject in six minutes."*

■ **Does "saying it in six" make you *more* excited about
your original idea or proposal—or does it make you suspect
that you oversold yourself on it when you were just
thinking about it?**

— *Frankly, this could go either way. By shortening a message, distilling it, you can "see it" far more accurately. A
weak idea will fall apart when you clear out the sur-
rounding undergrowth. A powerful idea gains strength by
briefing it.*

■ **Do you feel that you've really cut your message to the
bone—that only the strongest material remains?**

— *Here's a good way to find out. Pick up your colored Hi-
liter and do what comes naturally. If your inclination is to
highlight something in every sentence, or the whole sentence, you're close to the bone.*

■ **Do you like the "shock value" of it?**

— *Most experienced speakers find the six-minute speech is
like diving into a cold pool. There's no "warm up" time.*

Wham! You're into it. But "the fast start" is precisely what business audiences like the most.

Here's an important point: the rationale for the six-minute message is urgency. You've got something so important to tell your audience that you want to get it to them as fast— almost as telegraphically—as possible. The "shock value" is instrumental to the atmosphere of your message. It's urgent—it cries out for their attention. You want your audience to sit up and take notice.

SHORT TAKE

Two advertising executives were discussing their experiences in the business: **"Once when I was in a meeting, it dawned on me that I was in the same meeting 20 years before."**

His partner nodded thoughtfully and added, **"Or in the same meeting for 20 years."**

—from the New York Times
Advertising Column,
October 5, 1994

CHAPTER 8

Two Very **Different** Ways to "Say It in Six"

*I*t's Interactive Time Again!

The next chapter is a six-minute speech all proofed and ready for delivery. It even has the props and audio/visual cued in.

The script was developed from recent articles in the business press and a series of face-to-face interviews with pharmacists in Chicago and Milwaukee.

Beyond that, it's merely an exercise. The brand name is made up. The numbers are loosely based on estimates by the pharmacists.

So, here's where you come in: Imagine that you are on the board of directors of a big pharmaceutical firm. A gutsy vice-president gets up and makes an important presentation to you.

Your only obligation: Keep an open mind. Let your imagination help you paint the scene. Reserve your judgment until the very end.

Most companies would shudder at the thought of a six-minute presentation "to the board." How about you? Read this chapter before you answer.

Presenting to the Board—in Six Minutes

> IN EXACTLY SIX MONTHS,
> OUR PATENTS ON OUR MOST
> PROFITABLE BRAND WILL
> EXPIRE FOREVER . . .
> THE BRAND IS PERSANON.
>
> ON THE DAY THAT
> OUR PATENTS EXPIRE,
> GENERIC MANUFACTURERS WILL
> ENTER THE MARKET WITH THEIR
> VERSION OF OUR PRODUCT
> <u>AND</u> <u>EAT</u> <u>US</u> <u>ALIVE</u>.

Good morning. This is a Burning Issue for this company. Can everybody see it?

The V.P. (Marketing) stands before the Board of Directors of a large pharmaceutical company. She pinpoints each word of the burning issue with a small laser pointer. The subject appears on an electronic copy board.

I hope I haven't startled anybody with this news. The facts *are* unsettling. Let me give you the only ones that are essential for you to know.

She presses a button on the electronic copy board. The message on the screen is reduced, copied, printed, and delivered in hard-copy form to the bottom of the screen. She walks over, picks it up, and tapes it to the front wall. The screen goes blank. She moves close to her audience.

Persanon now has a 45 percent share of market. It has been the leader in its category for the past 15 years. It accounts for over half of our net profits.

When the generics enter Persanon's market, our brand share will drop to around 12 percent. And our *net profits* will drop by more than the loss of market share. So, we're facing up to a 60 percent profit loss.

We have racked our brains to find some kind of response.

But *what?*

Virtually all of our actions are constrained by the Food and Drug Administration. We can't get an extension on our patents. And there is no way on earth that we can protect them.

We are clearly on the defensive.

This forced us to rethink our situation, and take a longer view.

*She returns to the Burning Issue posted on the front wall and draws a red circle around the word **"Persanon."***

This, I think we'll agree, is *our immediate concern.* But it's also the "trigger" for our long-term concern. It's what triggered us into the reality of what we see facing us— not just six months from now, but years from now.

The problem is not in the product. The problem is in the process. That is, the process of patents expiring and cheaper products—rip-offs, really—moving in and taking over the market.

What's happening to Persanon will happen again and again with other products as other patents expire.

We must find a way to work within the process *without* getting skinned alive. And the solution must work now *and* into the future.

Does everybody agree with that premise?

All right. With *that* as a point of view, I'd like to plunge right into the specifics of what we're recommending today.

She pauses for a beat or two.

We believe that we should get our laboratories working around the clock to develop our own generic version of Persanon—and that, with your approval, we should start just as soon as possible.

Our recommended timetable is to introduce our own generic to the market no later than 90 days from now. That means we must get FDA approval within 60 days. We're on a fast track.

But if we can do it—we will have our own generic on the market 90 days *before* any other generic is allowed to be there. A three-month head start!

What we are doing is not new to industry, but it is new to *our* industry. It is called . . .

She writes **"Preempting the Competition"** *on the electronic copy board.*

. . . *preempting the competition.* Here's why this is so important to us right now. In the pharmaceutical business, there is a basic principle which is so simple that it almost sounds like a slogan. *The first generic to reach the market wins the market.* Actually, it's just common sense. Assuming all generics are equal, people will buy the generic that offers the cheapest price *first.*

She writes **"We'll Be First"** *on the electronic copy board.*

We'll be first. And since we originated the leading brand in the category, our generic product should pick up a bigger share of market than we've ever had—probably 65 percent—and we'll have it almost immediately.

She writes, **"65 Percent Share of Market—Immediately"** *on the electronic copy board.*

I can read your faces. You are saying, "We are simply cannibalizing Persanon's market with a cheaper product. What's so great about that?"

You're absolutely right! That's exactly what we are doing. But there's one thing to remember: *It's still our market!*

*She writes **"It's Still Our Market"** on the electronic copy board.*

And, being the leader, we should be able to price our generic aggressively—at about two thirds of Persanon's price. That's still highly profitable.

*She writes **"We'll Stay Profitable"** on the electronic copy board.*

In short, we are operating within *the process* to protect ourselves. We cannot protect our patents. *But we can protect our competitive advantage.*

In case you're wondering, there is nothing in the world that says we can't bring out a new product 90 days prior to the expiration of our own patent.

*She writes **"We're In the Clear"** on the electronic copy board.*

This strikes me as a pretty positive list for a company that was about to "be eaten alive."

She punches up the entire list on the electronic copy board. All points are illuminated.

> **PREEMPTING THE COMPETITION.**
> **WE'LL BE FIRST.**
> **65 PERCENT SHARE OF MARKET—IMMEDIATELY.**
> **IT'S STILL OUR MARKET.**
> **WE'LL STAY PROFITABLE.**
> **WE'RE IN THE CLEAR.**

She lets them read the board and then punches out 10 hard copies. The machine makes the copies as she walks toward the group.

There are other benefits to this preemptive strategy. Important ones. It will enable us to avoid mass firings and keep our laboratories and production facilities working.

That should be good for morale.

And Wall Street should take note that we are going to fight for our stockholders in every way that's smart and legal.

She returns to the machine and scoops up the hard copies. She gives one to each of the directors. She's talking as she hands out the sheets.

To tell you the truth, I've boiled this presentation down *many* times. I just knew that it was far more important for you to interact with each other than for me to stand up here and talk.

Of course we need your blessings before we can take the next step. So, let's have some coffee together. I'm eager to hear your reactions.

She moves briskly from the front of the room toward the coffee, picks up a cup, and turns to talk to one of the directors.

*Her entire presentation has taken **less than** six minutes.*

A Complex Medical Presentation Comes Alive in Six Minutes. The R_x for Your Next Meeting?

What you can learn from the preceding six-minute presentation:

1. An astonishing amount of information can be communicated in six minutes—provided the structure is strong and the language is lean.

2. You can handle a very important presentation in six minutes. In fact, it becomes *more* important because it is unencumbered with the *clutter* that makes most speeches ordinary.

3. The six-minute structure works:

   A. The *Burning Issue* jumps right out at you.
   B. The *Overview* starts the second that the presenter draws the red circle around *Persanon*. It continues for 45 seconds. It is so clearly defined that she can ask for agreement on her analysis of the situation before she moves on.
   C. The *Idea Made Tangible (IT)* starts immediately after the Overview. There are no wordy transitions. She names the idea—*preempting the competition*. She uses a dramatic audio/visual device to make the idea visual—and later makes her idea tangible (with hard copies).
   D. The *Payoff*. She nails the cost/benefit requirements with a few key figures, then adds some other benefits for good measure.
   E. She ends graciously with an invitation to "Interactive Coffee."

4. There is a sense of *urgency* about this presentation that gives validity to the six-minute length. She feels strongly about the subject. She wants to get moving with her idea.

5. She moves around, but always with a reason. She seems perfectly natural.

6. Her sentences are short, often telegraphic.

7. She covers a lot of ground, but she doesn't seem hurried. She has rehearsed this presentation many times, but she *hasn't* memorized it.

8. This is a very businesslike presentation, but it has a *presence*. That's an undefinable word, but you sure know it when you see it.

9. ***What can you add?***

—How did you feel about it as a member of the board?
—How did you feel about it as an observer?
Suggestion: Go back and scan the six-minute presentation in light of the observations made here. Have we missed anything?

_____

_____

_____

_____

_____

_____

_____

_____

_____

_____

_____

_____

SHORT TAKE

Juries remember only 60 percent of what they're told.

WHY?

Answer: The case isn't about them. No matter how hard they try, people have trouble paying attention to presentations that aren't about them.

Moral: Talk to the self-interest of your audience at all times.

The Impact of Say It in Six *on Meetings of the Past*

What meetings used to be:	**Where you're taking them:**

What meetings used to be:

- Social gatherings, gossip sessions, authorized chitchat.

- *Information dispensers. That is, meetings "for information only." No action required.*

- "Habits"—such as the office manager's weekly status review.

- *Political manueuvers. A chance for department heads to keep an eye on each other—see who's getting the favors and who's not.*

- Ego platforms, where everybody was encouraged to "say something."

- *Slow, ambling pace. Much daydreaming. People wandered in and out.*

Where you're taking them:

- Fast, "plunge in" starts. Lean language. Short, stubby sentences.

- *Only the information needed to make a sound decision is presented.*

- Meetings are reserved for "Burning Issues" only.

- *Only the active "players" attend. Everybody has a specific responsibility. There is no time for politics.*

- All comments must contribute to the decision. Self-promotion is dealt with summarily.

- *Solid six-minute presentation followed by interaction until decision is reached. Meeting is expected to be over in less than 30 minutes.*

75

Open Meeting at Brush Creek: Another Way to "Say It in Six"

Ever since the notion of interaction arrived via cyberspace, people have been having "open meetings." There is no structure, no agenda, no program. One thing just leads to another, and pretty soon—an idea is hatched, or a solution is born.

It is not unlike group therapy, or what used to be called "brainstorming."

The six-minute speech has often proved useful in these freewheeling and sometimes scattershot forums. The speaker speaks for less than six minutes *in toto*, but the audience gets down to business faster without losing a jot of creative vitality.

To see how it works, drop everything for a few minutes and come to Brush Creek—a shopping center with a real Burning Issue and a dire need for about six minutes' worth of discipline.

Organizing Chaos:

It is a large, plain meeting room. Six round tables look a little lost in the vast space.

Men and women are filtering in now. Well dressed. Middle-aged, for the most part. There isn't much conversation. There's a security guard at the door checking identification.

Mrs. Helen Hawley, chairperson of the Brush Creek Merchants' Association, is shouting instructions from the front of the room. "Just seat yourself at a table—any table."

Forty merchants and store managers have been invited to this "extremely important" special meeting. It looks as if more than 30 will show up.

Slowly, all of the tables are occupied. As the people sit down, they notice a big paper bag in the middle of each table. The bags are filled with art supplies—Magic Markers, crayons, colored pencils, and one complete set of cheap watercolors. There is also a two-by-three-foot pad of heavy drawing paper at each of the six tables.

The mood is uncertain.

Mrs. Hawley starts precisely at 2 P.M.

"As the notice said, you'll be out of here in two hours. What the notice didn't say is that you will be doing all the work."

The body language of the audience suddenly becomes more attentive.

The Burning Issue of Brush Creek

"Brush Creek is dying. We've all felt it. Business is down for the third straight year. Our old customers have left us. And we're not replacing them. Everyone in this room has seen the problem—and felt the problem. We're simply not making it."

The Overview

"There are many reasons—but mainly two. No, *three*. As you know, downtown has been completely rebuilt—and it's gorgeous. Our oldest customers seem to be moving back there—and the downtown stores are making a big play for them. It's almost like a return to your childhood, if you're the right age. Reason two: Our youngest customers are heading out to the newer malls—miles from here. And third, and most important, we've lost our identity. We're somewhere between downtown and the new fashion malls. People don't know how to think of us anymore."

The audience is attentive. Nobody is resisting Mrs. Hawley's analysis.

The Idea Made Tangible

Mrs. Hawley then moves into the "idea" section of her meeting—picking up a large piece of cardboard that's been resting against a wall. It has words on it, but the audience can't see them.

"We need to *position* Brush Creek. By that I mean we have to give it a new identity that will make people want to shop here again. It must be brief, appealing, *and competitive.*

"What I'm holding here is a positioning statement that is 50 years old. I found it in one of the old storerooms we don't use anymore. Somebody wrote this a long time ago—but it's an identity that worked during its time."

She holds up the old board and reads from it:

BRUSH CREEK:
FASHION CENTER OF THE ELITE.
Brush Creek presents the finest shops
in the Midwest. With its distinctive Aztec
architecture, this unique community
offers an exotic shopping experience
you will never forget.

"Not bad for fifty years ago, is it?" Some of the merchants are smiling now, remembering.

Mrs. Hawley moves among the six tables, holding the board over her head so that everybody can read it.

"You can learn from this," she says. "Keep it simple, keep it short, make it distinctive."

"Should it be true?" someone asks.

"If it works, we'll make it true," Mrs. Hawley replies without missing a beat.

She places the cardboard gently against the wall.

"The people sitting around your table are your teammates. If you don't know them, shake hands."

There is a rustle of activity as people lean across tables.

"I'm going to give you some positioning boards just to get you started. One to a table. There is absolutely no pride of authorship in these positionings. They were done by my staff. Edit them up or down—any way you want."

She gathers some fresh-looking boards from against the wall and doles them out—one per team.

A game-playing atmosphere is beginning to sneak into the room, and the noise level is encouraging.

"Now, here's what I want you to do. Each team will create three positioning boards to add to the one I just gave you. You'll find all kinds of art supplies on every table—and a big tablet full of poster-weight sheets. Those are for *your* positionings."

Mrs. Hawley has done the first three steps of the six-minute structure and done them well.

■   Her audience knows "the Burning Issue."

■   It has heard a candid and concise overview of the situation.

■   It has been briefed on an "idea" to attach to the problem. Mrs. Hawley has made the idea "tangible" (and emotional) by dramatically showing the 50-year-old board she found in her storeroom.

A little later, Mrs. Hawley's voice carries across the room. "If you have four positionings on your table, raise your hand."

Hands go up.

"Now I want you to get out of your chairs and move, as a team, to another table. *Leave all the work you have just done behind you.*"

"I don't believe it," a voice says.

"Just trust me on this, will you," Mrs. Hawley says evenly. The teams move slowly to different tables, all of which are littered with papers and magic markers.

"All right. Is every team at a new table?" Murmurs indicate yes.

"Take a careful look at the four positionings at your new table and improve on them any way you can. Make them shorter. Sharpen the language. Do whatever your experience tells you will make them more effective."

The teams start to work.

"Then . . ."

A mild groan fills the room.

"Then . . . write a slogan or theme line for each positioning. Something short and punchy that we can use in every ad we run. If you have a graphic idea that brings the theme line to life, sketch it in. Don't be bashful. Stick figures are perfect."

The activity heats up again. Every team is working hard.

"How many people *like* doing this?" Maybe half the people raise their hands.

"The reason we're doing this is because sociologists have found that the best way to create new information is to bring bright people like you together in new and different ways. When you get rid of the old boundaries and turn people loose, you facilitate change. People discover all kinds of creativity they never knew they had before."

The audience looks at her with renewed interest.

"Okay, everybody, you've got one more table to go. I want you to get up and move, as a team, to a table you haven't occupied before. *Leave your work behind you.*"

The teams go willingly now. They move quickly to a different table.

"There are six tables in the room. You should be sitting at your third table. All you have to do at your third table is select the best positioning board and the theme line that goes with it—and then improve the board and its theme line by at least 50 percent.

"That should be easy for a bunch of savvy marketers like yourselves."

With this instruction, the decibel level in the room reaches a new high. Arguments break out at several tables. Colored pencils flash across the positionings as changes are made.

"Does each team have a captain?" Mrs. Hawley asks, knowing the answer is no.

"Appoint a captain. Each captain will be responsible for presenting his or her winning positioning statement and theme line to the rest of us."

"Team captains—I'll give you a few minutes to rehearse your presentations."

Now, for the first time, there's a definite feeling of competition in the room.

As the team captains present their winning boards and theme lines, a chorus of voices fills the room.

"Charlie, there's your theme line."

"Look, our idea made the finals. How 'bout that?"

When the six recommended positionings and theme lines are placed side by side along the wall, Mrs. Hawley says, "I think all of you deserve a round of applause." The crowd doesn't hesitate to applaud itself.

The Payoff

 "Before you leave, I want you to know the payoff on your work. We'll test the winning ideas on the people who should be shopping at our stores—and we'll keep you posted on our progress. Some of you will be heading committees. Then, we'll take the absolute winner of all of the work you've done here today and build our fall promotion around it. With a good fall and a modest improvement in our holiday season, we'll have Brush Creek back on its feet by the first of next year. We'll have to increase our direct mail and advertising by less than 10 percent—but that should be more than covered by a solid gain in business. We've got no alternative but to go for it!"

The Interactive Close

At that moment, two men from the local deli rush into the room, loaded with boxes.

"I didn't think you were going to make it. Folks, the refreshments have arrived."

Mrs. Hawley starts handing out cold drinks and potato chips.

The merchants start talking among themselves. The mood is up-beat, and the work on the wall is drawing a lot of comments.

As the bottles pop open, it looks like nobody has the slightest intention of leaving.

You'll have to admit that this has been a very unusual meeting—a far cry from the old "clothesline" meetings where people sat passively and listened to somebody talk. Here, we've had the audience thrashing about—not really knowing what was going to happen next, doing things they didn't quite understand. What do you make of it?

Take six minutes to note your observations. Would you want to try a meeting like this? Dig back into the meeting for some insights. Then we'll compare notes on the next two pages.

*T*en Insights from the Showdown at Brush Creek

1. It was a two-hour meeting, but Mrs. Hawley spoke for less than six minutes. Four minutes and thirty seconds, to be exact. Just enough to keep things on track.

2. That means her audience was participating—*interacting*—95 percent of the time. And that means the likelihood of her audience remembering the meeting (and its results) is inordinately high. According to the experts, we remember over 90 percent of what happens in a highly participatory meeting.

3. Creating teams is a smart technique. Put a person on a team and he or she usually becomes a team player. It certainly reduces the danger of heckling.

4. Mrs. Hawley knows the value of keeping people on the move. By moving people from table to table, she kept the meeting *active* rather than passive.

5. By following the structure of the six-minute speech (even though she didn't make a speech), she gave a semblance of order to what could have been a chaotic meeting.

6. A game-playing atmosphere not only encourages an audience to lower all barriers to an idea, it challenges them to see if they can play (and maybe even *win*).

7. The technique of getting people to improve each other's work does two worthy things:

    A. It brings additional brains into play and invariably makes the work better.

    B. It broadens the feeling of accomplishment. When a voice yells out, "Look, our idea made the finals," it is a moment of pride for that team—but it is also a good moment for all of the *other* people who made contributions.

8. Nothing gets an audience involved like the hint of competition.

9. If you're asking people to do something that sounds irrational (like moving from table to table), it's always advisable to give them a rational reason for doing it (sociologists say it produces creative results).

10. When decision time rolls around, you'll find it's much easier to get an approval when the people are voting on their own work.

SHORT TAKES

Every morning in Africa, a gazelle wakes up knowing it must run faster than the lion or be killed. Every morning a lion awakens knowing it must outrun the slowest gazelle or starve to death. It doesn't matter if you are a lion or a gazelle. When the sun comes up, you'd better be running.

—Anonymous

You have to work smarter, you have to work faster, or someone will overrun you.

—Nina DiSesa,
executive vice president and
executive creative director,
McCann-Erickson, New York

CHAPTER 9

The **Style** of the Six-Minute Speaker

- Starts fast. You know who's got the floor now.

- Speaks at least 150 words a minute. Doesn't worry about talking too fast.

- Starts where most "speeches" finally get going: about halfway through.

- *Almost* memorizes.

- Never equivocates.

- Never gives choices.

- Never leaves any doubt about his or her position.

- Rivets people with eye contact.

- Stands, if possible. If sitting, never slouches. Sits *up*—like a TV commentator.

- Gestures only when making a point. *Everything has a purpose.*

- Regards six minutes as a deadline. Seldom goes over.

How about a Role Model for Your Six-Minute Speech?

If you were to seek out the perfect role model for your first six-minute speech, you'd have a hard time finding a better icon than David Brinkley.

Brinkley may be the best TV journalist who ever lived (though some old-line news junkies would insist that Edward R. Murrow shares that distinction).

David Brinkley has surely had more imitators and clones than any other TV newscaster who ever faced a camera.

One quote about him, made by his producer Reuven Frank, pretty well sums up his greatest talent: "He gets more information into 100 words than anyone I've ever worked with."

The *New York Times* says it a bit differently. "Mr. Brinkley's extraordinary accomplishment has been not to talk too much. He has the knack for the succinct phrase that sums up the situation."

Indeed he does. Brinkley is sometimes so terse in his delivery that his guests seem startled by it. Try this—from *This Week with David Brinkley* on ABC. (The show has been running, weekly, since November 15, 1981.) Here is how he opened his interview with a high-ranking U.S. diplomat:

> "We're troubled by what's happening in Bosnia. You're just back. What's happening?"

Once inside of a subject, he doesn't let go. Recently the secretary of transportation was a guest on the Brinkley show. Five USAir planes had crashed in the previous five years. The secretary was squirming under some of Brinkley's crisp, cutting questions. Finally, he said, "You don't want to pronounce a death sentence on the airline, do you?"

Brinkley shot back, "It just killed an awful lot of people."

David Brinkley is the master of the conjunctive dash. That is—just say it—don't pretty it up—dig it out—make it clear—make it simple—tell us—let's move on.

As a result, his famous speech patterns have an urgency that is seldom heard in this era of mellifluous announcers. Listening to Brinkley is like hearing a baritone jackhammer—breaking things up so you can understand them more easily.

Even the shortest of sentences will get the Brinkley clarifying treatment. "See you again—next week."

Listen to him deliver one of his one-minute essays at the end of his program. You can almost hear the pauses in the words below. Read the following aloud. Even if you don't try to imitate his style, you can almost hear his voice chopping the text into neat little chunks.

> "Here in Washington, members of the House of Representatives enjoy a privilege that is denied to all of us and envied by most of us.
>
> "When a member makes a speech on the house floor, stenographers take down every word—type it up—then it's printed in the daily Congressional Record.
>
> "That is, it's printed after the member has gone over it, corrected it himself, changed its errors, removed its bad grammar, and taken out everything that—for some political reason—he wishes he had not said.
>
> "Receivers of the Record get a version of what was said—corrected, purified, pasteurized—and usually fairly dull and often pumped by 25 to 30 percent.
>
> "Now, they say, this will stop. Hereafter, the Record will print only the truth—what they really said.
>
> "But of course there will still be the baloney, but maybe a little less.
>
> "When you live in Washington, you take what little truth you can get—where you can get it."

A droll smile appears, along with a slightly arched eyebrow, producing a look of satisfaction that says, "Well, I gave it to 'em again—and they damn well deserve it."

Brinkley says he hates the sound of his own voice—but it is probably the most quickly recognized voice on the airwaves. Not for the texture of it—but for the unmistakable *cadence* of it.

Break it up. Break it down. Make it clear. No baloney.

Many people remember Brinkley for his co-anchoring days on NBC with fellow newscaster Chet Huntley (Huntley always said that Brinkley could read the dictionary and make it sound provocative.) For all of the famous stories they covered night after night, one ritual ceremony seems to have left the deepest impression:

"Good night, David."

"Good night, Chet."

Brinkley thought it was phoney and theatrical. But the viewers liked it. And so it stayed. "Made them more human," the producer said. Brinkley probably scoffed and said nothing.

Besides always knowing when to say nothing, what else can we learn from the long career of David Brinkley? What can we learn that you can use in your first six-minute speech? There have to be dozens of characteristics of the Brinkley style that will work almost as well for you. Let's nail a few.

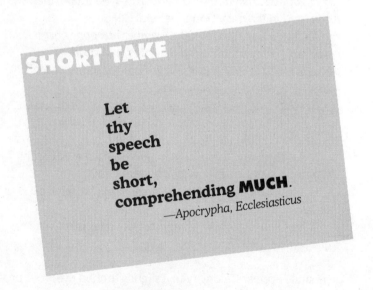

SHORT TAKE

Let
thy
speech
be
short,
comprehending **MUCH**.
—Apocrypha, Ecclesiasticus

David Brinkley's Style Can Help You "*Say It in Six*"

1. Get right into the guts of it. Go for the Burning Issue *instantly.*

2. Make conciseness your trademark. Use short, stubby words. Don't worry about conjunctives. Keep your sentences spare.

3. Don't allow yourself to get entangled in long, suffocating discussions. Distill the arguments—and move on.

4. Be polite to everybody, but don't cotton up to anybody. Other people recognize it.

NOTE: Brinkley has the remarkable ability to come across as gracious and welcoming—and then pound a question right into the guest's heart.

5. If you've got a wit, use it. If there's a sting to it, so be it.

6. Concentrate on what your audience wants to know, *not* on what you want to talk about.

7. Write like people talk. Speak like people talk. Avoid the literary style.

8. Practice making things *clearer* by deleting words, *not* by adding.

9. Don't be afraid to smile at yourself. People hate a pompous ass.

10. Keep cool even when things jangle your nerves.

11. Crystallize, crystallize. If you see an idea lurking behind a dense cluster of language, pull it out and hold it up for the world to see.

12. Don't be afraid to ask the hard questions—or give the hard answers. The six-minute speech relies on candor.

13. Don't be afraid to develop your own style. But it must communicate quickly. The last thing anybody wants to hear is a plodder.

14. Stop when you're finished. Don't just fill the time with words. Rehashers can drive you crazy.

David Brinkley has been honing his style for over half a century. He may retire soon. Be sure to sit down and savor him—as one of the great communicators—before he signs off.

SHORT TAKE

We will all die of information overload unless we find a way to say things better and shorter. If we can't do both, then shorter is better.
—Edward Stephens, former dean of the S.I. Newhouse School of Public Communications, Syracuse University

SHORT TAKE

Pretend that you're hearing these words:
Madonna
Shark
Rifle
Roller coaster
Baby
Roses
Sailboat
Alligator
Umbrella

Now, pretend that you're hearing these words:
Paradigm
Tautology
Generic
Eclectic
Conglomeration
Philosophy

Which list did you see in your mind's eye? Which list did you have trouble seeing?

There's a lesson here. Use "picture words" in your six-minute speech and you will be remembered. "Picture words" register quickly.

Avoid words that pass through your mind's eye without leaving snapshots behind. They register slowly—or not at all.

SHORT TAKE

Nervousness occurs when you are deeply concerned about yourself.

Nervousness is very selfish. You're afraid you'll be boring. You're just plain afraid . . . mostly for yourself.

How about being deeply concerned about *the audience's problem* that you have been asked to address? How about being deeply fearful for *their* welfare?

The sooner you transfer the deep concern you feel for yourself to the deep concern you should be feeling for your audience, the sooner you'll be over your nervousness.

CHAPTER 10

Nipping
Nervousness
in the Bud

*E*xperts say, *"Nervousness is the fear of rejection." That is unmitigated hooey.* Audiences do not "reject" speakers. How many speakers have you seen *rejected*? That is, tossed out—reviled—banished from the premises?

A speaker, in order to be *rejected*, would have to be so obnoxious, so revolting, so distasteful, so downright miserable that he or she should wear a "kick me" sign.

Audiences don't *reject* speakers. If they don't care for them, they simply start daydreaming.

Here is the answer: Bundle up all of the charts and chalk and clippings and Magic Markers and photos and cartoons you can find. Take 'em all. Whenever the audience starts to daydream on you, draw a picture—make a graph—write some-  body's name on the blackboard—read a headline—stand on a chair—give somebody a high five—act upon something that will force the audience to refocus its attention *back on you*.

Audiences think faster than you talk. If they get bored with what you're saying, change the subject—*but do it visually—that's the only way to get them concentrating on you again.* Make a scene they cannot resist. And forget, forever, about being rejected. It's not going to happen—so why on earth should it make you nervous?

*U*nderstanding Where and When Nervousness Strikes

In a six-minute presentation, the chances of your being nervous are *far less* than during a long, complicated speech. It stands to reason. You're following a simple structure rather than an ornate outline. And there's obviously less time—and less opportunity— for you to be unnerved by something unexpected.

However . . .

There are *possibilities* for nervousness in a six-minute presentation, and we're going to attack those "possibility points."

In your experience, where is nervousness most likely to occur? At what points in a presentation?

In a six-minute presentation, "at the start" is very definitely number one.

1.   **At the start.** This means just before you start to speak and just after you've begun. There is a span of about three minutes— with the actual start somewhere in the middle of the span— that must be declared critical. One reason: The audience may include people you have never seen before—and they may be totally in the dark about you. So, there's a kind of "void" that's waiting to be filled. That "void" can cause nervousness.

This is not as likely in a meeting held inside your organization—where everybody is supposed to know everybody else—but it happens. You walk into a room and see strangers. Your nerves jump. If you are giving a six-minute presentation for the first time, you have reason to feel even more unsettled.

Maybe these "strangers" have never experienced a six-minute presentation before. Maybe they'll equate "brevity" with "superficiality." Maybe they were expecting the usual 20-minute harangue. (Did you know that the average business meeting in the United States lasts an hour and a half!) Maybe

94

a six-minute presentation is too much of a "leap forward" to expect a conservative organization to take in stride. Maybe, maybe, maybe . . . "maybe's" have a way of causing nervousness.

Let's pin down the other three "possibility points" for nervousness and then hurry back to number one with some "fixes."

2. **When you feel your audience is slipping away from you.** Every speaker has had this nerve-rattling experience. It can happen anywhere in a presentation, but it's most likely to happen when your audience has had a chance to "size you up" and make a judgment of sorts. They haven't "counted you out" yet—but they're beginning to drift on you. In a six-minute presentation, this can happen about halfway through. You know the signs. Eye contact can become difficult. Body language can start to tell you things. Feet can start to shuffle on the floor. Noses can start to sniffle. You're losing your audience—you can *feel* it—you can *hear* it—and restless people can make you fidgety. What can you do? Just be patient for a second or two—we're coming right back.

3. **When your memory betrays you and you're lost within your own presentation.** Everybody has had this feeling, too. Your mind decides to take a "break." You can't find anything. And nervousness settles in like an unwelcome houseguest. We've got a graphic answer for this "possibility"—and you're going to love it.

4. **When you fear for your audio/visual equipment. You suddenly realize that if your A/V goes out, you're toast.** Some of the new electronic A/V equipment isn't nearly as simple—or as portable—or as foolproof—as the full-color brochures claim. Just *reading* about some of this new stuff can give a speaker a headache. Hold on. Advice is close at hand.

*N*ow, Let's Strike Back at Nervousness

The most likely place for nervousness: at the start of your presentation. If you like the idea of "Say It in Six" and you say, "By golly, why not?"—here's what you should do:

> *Before the meeting, call up a few close colleagues who will also be attending—and tell them exactly what you will be doing, and why. Tell them how you feel—and you'd really welcome their support. If they can't give you that, tell them an open mind will do nicely.*

This small preconditioning step will help you launch into your six-minute presentation without worrying about shock waves when you finish. You may also want to include your boss in this preliminary step—but we'll leave that entirely up to you.

Another "must" for minimizing nervousness at the start: Start like a thoroughbred breaking out of the gate and don't look back. Put the Burning Issue on a board where everybody can see it and let your enthusiasm carry you. Use the short, blunt, no-baloney words we've talked about. Watch for facial reactions. You'll know immediately if you've hit a nerve. If all systems are operating properly, you'll find that you have left nervousness behind—and your enthusiasm is carrying you along.

One final reminder for beating nervousness from the start: You're not standing up there, moving your mouth and working your

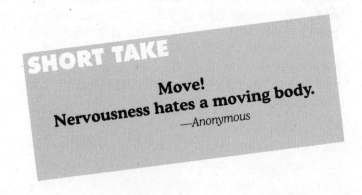

SHORT TAKE

Move!
Nervousness hates a moving body.
—Anonymous

brain, to make the first six-minute speech in history. Avoid the idea of "making a speech." What you're doing is laying a solid foundation for the decision that is sure to follow. That's what this is all about: getting the proposition into the clear so that an important decision will take place later. Maybe a few minutes later, maybe longer. But your job is to make the right decision *easy*—not to dazzle everybody with your six-minute footwork.

Somehow, you're losing your audience.  Every speaker knows this feeling. It's a little like nausea. The audience was with you a minute ago. You saw their eyes, felt their interest. Now, they're somewhere else. What happened? Where are they? *Their* boredom is making you nervous. You're into the fourth minute of your six-minute presentation, and your audience has blanked out—listening but not listening. If this were a traditional speech—say, 20 minutes or so—you'd stop and start asking questions. But you've got about two minutes to go. You're just coming into the *Payoff* section—full of cost savings and major benefits to your audience. *Keep going.* Just turn up your presentation techniques and finish strong. (Remember Ronald Reagan asserting himself in the primary campaign of 1980? "I am paying for this microphone!") At least they will have heard your full story—and they'll realize that you have thought it all the way through.

If someone breaks in before you've finished, of course you'll want to deal with whatever the issue is. It could be something minor. But a six-minute presentation is so tightly and cogently organized that you really don't want to break into it prematurely. There's also this to consider: If you complete your presentation— knowing that you had some glazed eyeballs a few minutes back— you'll know exactly where to focus your attention when you move into the discussion phase.

Here's the point: Having a plan for *any* eventuality—knowing what you will do in any situation—will do more to help you control nervousness than any pill or potion you've ever heard of.

When your memory fails. It's hard for a presenter to get lost in a six-minute presentation—but if it happens, it could activate your nervous system in a hurry. Well, never fear. We've got a safety net for you. It's called a "Palm Map," because it fits in the palm of your hand. It simply adds graphic detail to the basic structure which *never* changes. You merely glance at it—recognize the colors and pictures, and your memory comes roaring back to life. Also, your nerves subside. You don't have to be able to draw to use a "Palm Map." You don't have to be James Bond or know any secret color code. You simply have to take a close look at the graphic at the end of this chapter, then make your own "Palm Map." You'll find that just *having* this little memory aid will keep nervousness at bay.

What if the audio/visual equipment breaks down and nobody can fix it? Everybody has had this fear. The video could go berserk. The bulb could burn out in the projector. The slides could jam. The power could go out. Anything could happen, and you're about as high-tech as a doorknob. These days, the audio/visual equipment is so fancy that the speaker feels insignificant beside it. Without the A/V, the show is over—and the speaker stands there like a puppet who's just had his strings cut. Nervous? You're humiliated.

Some remedies:

■ Take a technician with you.

■ Be able to steam right on, A/V or no A/V. Actually, you should be able to do your six-minute presentation *on your own* no matter what happens. Let the power surge. Let the computer explode. You can carry on.

■ Have hard copies of what your A/V equipment was going to show. Move closer to your audience and talk from the hard copies—just as you were going to do with the A/V displays. Pass the hard copies around and let people get engaged with them. Let the mood change. Instead of a "show," you're *escorting* your audience through the visuals—getting their comments—and closing. Maybe not doing it the way you thought you would, but *closing* nonetheless.

Here's the hard truth of it: If you can't explain everything that your A/V equipment was supposed to illuminate, you're not prepared.

One thing you must *not* do: Don't stand on one leg and then the other—saying, "I'm sure everything will be fine in just a moment or two." This is a dead giveaway that the equipment knows more about the presentation than you do. This is *not* what you want your audience to take away from your presentation.

SHORT TAKE

Ever noticed how urgent messages are invariably short and sharp?

Get out!
Jump!
Hurry!
Run for your life!
Fire!
Save me!
Help!
Catch him!
Faster!
Watch out!
Duck!
Hold on!
Bar the door!
Get away!
Go for it!

THE PALM MAP

How the Palm Map Works: *Follow the structure of "Say It in Six" (as shown on page 34). Just add stick figures, or faces, or symbols, or key words—or all of the above—to jog your memory.*

This is a Palm Map for the trainee "Burning Issue" in chapter 5. Color the Burning Issue red, then add a sketch or two that tweaks your memory. In this case, a trainee is being yanked away by a competitor. The Overview suggests that attitudes have changed ("Me, Me, Me") and that young people think of themselves as products (in a box) to be sold to the highest bidder. The Idea Made Tangible ("IT") is represented by a new graduation certificate. The proposed program: make it tougher (trainee with more books and computer). Extend program from 8 to 12 weeks (8–12) And add a $5,000 bonus to make it more difficult to lure trainees away. You get the idea.

Stay with the basic structure, but add "little visuals" that clue your memory. Use lots of colors. Have fun with it.

The Palm Map shouldn't be more than 4" × 5" (unless you've got a very big hand). Glance at it from time to time if you need to. And you've got your own private safety net!

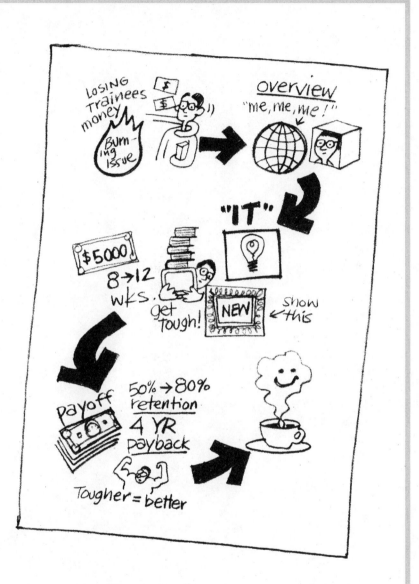

PART THREE

Special Delivery!

(In Six Minutes or Less)

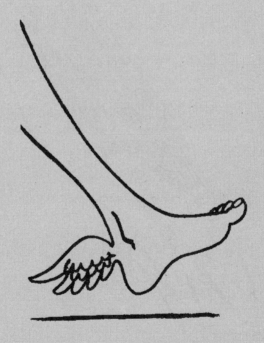

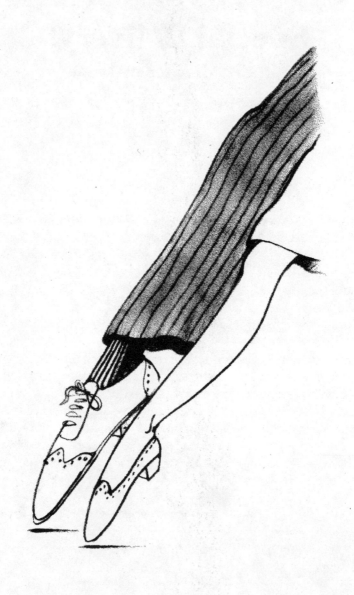

CHAPTER 11

Should Six-Minute Speeches Be Taken **Seriously?**

"**W**ho Goes to the Dance?"

You won't find a more intriguing plotline for a business drama than I discovered in Monterey, California.

In Hollywood, the premise would be described this way: The hungry and aggressive "young entrepreneurs" come seeking money and favors from the wily veterans of the financial community—called from this point forward, "deep pockets."

A tentative title: *Who Goes to the Dance—and Who Doesn't?*

Here's the way it works:

Every entrepreneur makes a six-minute presentation during the morning session—from 8:30 to noon. The audience is composed of bankers, venture capitalists, brokerage houses, and the like. Seasoned executives with "deep pockets." Most of the entrepreneurs need money—for everything from secondary offerings to "growing the business." Or, they may be planning to "go public" some day and they'd like to make a good impression on companies that recommend or buy stocks.

What we're talking about here *are very big stakes.*

The entrepreneurs have all taken suites in the hotel where the conference is being held—and they hope that the people with "deep pockets" will come calling in the afternoon and make a commitment. In other words, *"ask them to dance."*

Those companies that are left waiting at the front doors of their suites probably have only their six-minute presentations to blame.

They simply didn't come across as *attractive enough* to warrant a serious visit.

So, when the first entrepreneur steps up to make his presentation at 8:30 A.M., it's a pretty dicey moment. There's a timer in place with green, yellow, and red lights. And there's just about every type of audio/visual device that an aggressive, young entrepreneur might want.

The "deep pockets" people (115 of them) are all settled in their seats, ready to fill out their dance cards.

After sitting through two mornings of this high-stakes drama, and listening to no less than 39 six-minute presentations, I came away with a tote-bag full of impressions and observations that should be helpful when you make your first six-minute presentation.

Observations and Insights to Help You "Say It in Six"

- **Everything is accentuated in a six-minute presentation.** The audience is generally more alert—more "tuned in"—because it knows things will move quickly. So, the listening level is up—at least at the very start. Also, the six-minute presentation has to be simpler, more focused. Your audience is going to be more sensitive to what you have selected to leave in. As a result, things are going to show up in sharp relief—both good and bad. Here are a couple of examples. . . .

- **In a six-minute speech, undiluted candor can jump right out at you.** A young CEO was talking about his start-up company. "Look, we're willing to put our own money into this skins game," he said in dead earnestness. He flashed a slide on the screen. It looked like this:

  $4,900,000   YOU

  $5,700,000   US

Everybody got the message. Here was a guy who would put his money where his mouth is. He made a strong impression.

■ **Grievous errors can also jump out at you in six minutes.** A speaker took the platform and punched up an image on the screen. Here's exactly what it said:

OUR OBJECTIVE TODAY:

He went on to spell out his company's objective in coming to the meeting. At the end of his presentation, he repeated the slide—and announced that he felt he had achieved his objective. A less polite audience would have yelled out: *"What about our objective? Have you done anything about that?"*

Just because you're making a six-minute presentation doesn't mean that you're excused from talking to the audience's self-interest. At the very least, the speaker might have started with something like this:

"Let me give you some late news about my company that can open up a great opportunity for yours."

The minute you leave the audience out of your presentation, you're talking to yourself.

■ **Need money from the financial community? Say it in six!** I talked at some length to the CEO of a venture capital firm. I asked him what he thought of the six-minute format. "Perfect," he said without hesitation. "Investors get asked for money all the time," he said. "So, they develop short attention spans. They listen selectively—for key points.

"I want to hear some obvious things—size of company, market category, capital resources—but mainly I want to hear 'What's the basic business proposition that's driving this company?'

"Good CEOs are out there telling their story every day—to a variety of important audiences. But the truly exceptional ones are telling it in a clean, surgical way that I can grasp almost instantly—certainly within six minutes."

He was quick to add that the interactive time following the six-minute presentation was crucial.

"The process here [in Monterey] is terrific: The six-minute presentation puts a crystal-clear focus on a business issue which can only be resolved interactively, face-to-face. That's when you look at your notes [made during the six-minute presentations] and decide who will get a visit."

■ **Beware of sarcasm in a six-minute presentation. It could backfire.** One of the early six-minute speakers got up and said in his first breath: "I feel like one of those used-car salesmen on TV that has to talk fast." "Oh-oh," I said to myself. "This person is not happy." But his presentation moved along nicely. He wasn't talking fast. And he ended well short of his six minutes. Bravo, I thought. Presentation completed, he looked up at his audience and said, "Thank you for giving me this brief time." Then, he was gone. He still sounded ruffled. A small thing, you may say. And I'd agree, except for one point.

If I were a banker with "deep pockets," would I want to go visit a disgruntled officer in his hotel suite that afternoon? Would I take a chance on putting money in his firm—or would I rather put it with somebody who is cheery and confident?

■ **Don't let six minutes stop you from taking risks.** Here we have six precious minutes—and a bunch of gung ho entrepreneurs. I thought to myself, "Batten down the hatches. Prepare yourself to be blown right out of your seat."

Well, not exactly. Here's the way it went: The presentations started when the graphics appeared (usually 35 mm slides or transparencies). The images on the screen were awful or terrific, dull or colorful, static or animated, but when the images stopped—the presentations were over.

The overhead lights went up and down as the speakers came and went. It lulled the mind. I yearned for disruption. For all of the creativity represented by the speakers and their companies, I didn't see much derring-do. I didn't gasp in surprise or recoil in horror.

Six minutes is a long time. It certainly doesn't preclude a bit of showmanship. The audience doesn't expect you to be David Copperfield. But there's no law against "magic."

■ **In a business where you are supposed to be on "the leading edge," your audio/visual equipment better measure up to your image.** An overhead projector with black-and-white transparencies just won't do it (especially when you have to tell an associate, "next slide, please"). Nor will 35 mm slides being clicked through a noisy carousel projector at the back of the room. As one young woman remarked, "They just aren't hip."

A laptop computer, wired through a converter to a liquid crystal projector, will give you dazzling color, animation, ripple dissolves, and almost anything you want in the way of special effects. It looks like a different generation of equipment— and it is.

■ **A little high-tech language is fine, but all venture capitalists are not wired for words like "edutainment" and "bioformatics."** Another advantage of the six-minute speech: You can pare things down to their simplest possible terms. The result is often stunning language.

An example: A young Japanese CEO introduced his company as "Radiance" (which was a welcome change after hearing about "gigabytes"). He said, "We're in the wire replacement business. We're going to knock copper out of consideration."

Now, *there*—I thought—is a proposition to drive a company. My venture capitalist friend would like that.

■ **If you encounter troubles during your six-minute speech, don't tell us—don't show us—don't admit to anything**. Most of the speakers seemed self-assured. The nervous ones gave off little signals that were impossible to miss. One speaker stood behind the podium and brushed his foot back and forth—like a tap dancer, practicing. The microphone picked up his nervous shuffle and reminded people that he was itching to get off the stage.

Another speaker explained how he had been "on his deathbed" with a horrible case of the flu and hoped that he could survive his presentation. He went through it as smoothly as you please—and seemed to cough deliberately after he finished just to prove he wasn't fibbing.

Why use up precious time in a six-minute speech drawing attention to your own pathetic condition? Don't confess to anything! Never share your tale of woe with an audience. I hate to tell you like this, but they don't give a damn.

■ **Don't let them put you in the dark—especially in a six-minute speech.** There's a voice booming across the ball-room—pictures changing on the screen—and no speaker! Where's the speaker? Is the narrator behind a curtain some-where? No, there's the speaker—that dark, shadowy figure standing next to the screen in a pool of darkness!

Every financial officer at the meeting said that the communications skills of the presenter—particularly if it was a top officer—would have some influence on how the company itself was regarded. So why make him or her look like a spy whose identity is being kept a secret?

Check the lights before you start. Position a "baby spot" just above the speaker's area. And don't douse the lights when the slides come on. It obliterates the speaker and makes note-taking almost impossible. It's easy to find a "happy medium" where the screen *and* the speaker can be seen. They don't put Dan Rather in the dark for the approximate six minutes he's on camera every night. Why should they want to hide *you*?

Coming to this conference of six-minute speeches was refreshing, and I am indebted to the American Electronics Association for inviting me. When was the last time you went to a conference and said, "I didn't hear a single speaker who talked too long?" When did you ever hear 20 speakers *in one morning*, with a nice, long break in the middle?

There were a few terrific speakers. Some could have been better. All of them were "interesting" in the best sense of the word. But I have a definite feeling that the timer with the green, yellow, and red lights (especially that red light) may have played the biggest role of all.

SHORT TAKE

Watching a Senate judiciary hearing can show you exactly what *not* to *do* at your next presentation.

— **Don't** say you'll talk for six minutes and then yammer for 20.

— **Don't** *ever* let your meeting leader say, "Take 30 minutes . . . or as long as you need." Your audience will expire before your very eyes.

— **Don't** ask questions that are really long-winded speeches. Senators *love* to do this.

— **Don't** get peevish. It makes everybody hunker down and feel uncomfortable.

— **Don't** let your own self-interest show like a banner blowing in the wind.

— **Don't** talk while you're fumbling through a stack of papers. The audience will know you're vamping.

— **Don't** play politics (even if you're a politician). Audiences know baloney when they hear it.

WANTED:

EXECUTIVE BRIEFING DIRECTOR
TO MANAGE
INFORMATION FLOOD

DJ COMPANY, leader in field, seeks exceptional individual to abstract and analyze all data sources (newsletters, Internet, on-line, business forums, wire services, magazines, newspapers, et al.) for the specific needs of our executive staff. Must be able to deliver customized, oral briefings in six minutes or less.

Crisp, unflappable presentation style required. If interested, respond with one-page summary of your qualifications. Finalists will be asked to make six-minute presentations to executive staff.

The need for data-gathering and data-analyzing experts is growing exponentially. Will you be ready when an ad like this appears?

CHAPTER 12

Learning from the Greatest Six-Minute Speakers in the World

Sharing Secrets with the Toastmasters

Most people have heard of Toastmasters International. It is a venerable old club—dedicated to "speaking, listening, and thinking." Founded in 1924, it was chartered as a nonprofit educational institution in 1932. Over two million people have passed through its portals, which are now worldwide.

Rather than lumber you with a heavy-duty history of the organization, I decided to attend some of the 50,000 speaking contests that Toastmasters conducts each year—and see what I could learn that I could pass along to you.

Six Toastmaster Secrets

1. **Give your speakers specific, but reasonable, time limits. Make the time limits visible to the speaker, then enforce the limits decisively.**

   For the speaking competitions at Toastmasters, all contestants are expected to prepare their presentations to last no longer than *seven* minutes and be no shorter than *five* minutes. The green light goes on at five minutes, stays on until six. The yellow light then glows from six to seven minutes. After that, a red light blazes.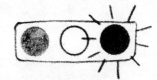

These lights come in different sizes, but they're all round and they all communicate instantly.

I asked Hugh Dunbar, a longtime officer of Toastmasters, about the time limitations and the need for them. He said the club has used time limits for as long as he could remember—and he has been around Toastmasters for 12 years. "We've found," he said, "that you must give each speaker adequate time to develop a subject—but you've also got to keep club meetings within a reasonable time frame. We think we're about right, in terms of time allowances, where we are now."

Where Toastmasters is now, in terms of actual time per speaker, is just over six minutes.

It is worth noting that no one at any of the meetings I attended—stopwatch in hand—complained about the time limits. However, most of the speakers admitted to being *aware* of the lights.

2.   There is a prevailing atmosphere of ritual and historical roots in Toastmasters meetings. It creates a kind of exhilaration that most corporations sadly lack.

Toastmasters does little, unexpected things that make you feel good about the organization. These "surprises" create a climate of civility and pride among the members that seems totally out of sync with the anger that erupts in many conference rooms. Here's an example of a Toastmasters "nice surprise":

At the very end of each five- to seven-minute speech, the speaker turns to the host or hostess, nods ever so slightly, and says, "Mr. Toastmaster . . ." (if a man happens to be chairing the meeting). This is a time-honored closing courtesy. The speaker is simply "giving the floor back" to the person in charge—but doing it with a style that respects the protocol of the past.

Your organization may have its own protocol, but maybe it's been neglected as managements have come and gone. If so, it wouldn't hurt to resurrect the old protocol, and try it in your next gathering. Every meeting needs a sense of style.

SHORT TAKE

Cicero said, "Brevity is the best recommendation of any speech."

But many of the ancient orators ignored his advice. They felt that every speech should have two objectives.

One: communicate a message.
Two: bring the audience together.

No more. If they don't buy number one, there's little hope for number two.

3.   Everyone who speaks at Toastmasters seems to get an enormous kick out of it. Imagine! Getting a kick out of speaking in public.

It can be the smallest, least significant announcement of the night, but whoever is making that announcement comes striding up to the front of the room and *sparkles*. (How long since you've heard that word used about a speaker in your corporation?) If there are stairs, speakers *bound* up them. If there's a podium, they lose no time in getting away from it. There's no groping for words at Toastmasters—no tremulous voices—no empty eyes. It's incredible. Everybody's alive!

One woman, explaining her reason for competing so energetically, said this:

> *"Look, I've got four kids at home—and I love them dearly, but they drive me nuts. I give them all my time while I'm with them, but when I'm at Toastmasters, I'm on my own time."*

NOTE: Toastmasters is a melting pot—all colors, all ages, all fields of endeavor. One contestant had retired from business, but he got up and made a ringing declaration for the conservative cause. (He said he's been competing for 40 years!) Another man, an Afro-American in his early 20s, got up and announced a David Letterman–style list of institutions that should "get over themselves." The state of Mississippi was near the top of the list.

The audience cheered both speakers.

4. **Attitudes about speaking are always positive—even when you lose.**

After one of the meetings, I went over to a contestant who had *not* won. He was a man in his early 50s and had obviously done a lot of speaking in his life. I told him he had been terrific. He thanked me with his big, booming voice and said, "You know, it just occurred to me that the object of this event is not to win—at least not for me. The object is to get yourself up off the couch and come over here and do it."

5. **There's a balance in great communications—of freedom and discipline. You must find that balance.**

People who join Toastmasters give themselves a forum to say whatever they damn well please (nobody messes with freedom of speech at these meetings), but you have to adopt a discipline or two before you gain the right to say whatever you like.

At Toastmasters, you don't just get up and compete. You have to make 10 different types of speeches—ranging from an "Icebreaker" to an "Inspirational." You get feedback after every speech. You have a mentor who counsels you along the way. After all 10 speeches, you can apply for Toastmaster certification—and if you get past that, you can compete, level by level by level, until you arrive at the world championships. There, in five to seven minutes, you may become the best speaker in the world.

Suggestion: Adopt some disciplines for your company's meetings. Give speakers the freedom to fail—but train them in the fundamentals before you turn them loose. You might want to start here, with some of the Toastmaster methods, or you might adopt the no-nonsense agenda in the next chapter.

6. ***Don't let your speakers get overwhelmed with electronic equipment.***

I was amazed to find that none of the Toastmasters contestants used audio/visual materials. I asked one of the judges if there was some rule against A/V aids. She said, "No," but she had seen only two speakers use them in the past nine years. This is a weakness, I think, although I did find a section on "visual aids" in the handbook.

There are two sides to this issue. I believe that visuals—that is, Ideas Made Tangible (IT)—increase memorability to a major degree. But Toastmasters is an organization that concentrates on the human voice. In fact, the handbook says that Toastmasters is dedicated "to making *oral communications* a worldwide reality." You really can't fault an organization that emphasizes the *human component* of communication, for that is exactly where most speakers need help.

Typical Toastmasters Competition — Notice how precisely everything is timed.

Schedule of Events

5:30 Toastmasters Gather

5:45 Contestant and Judges Briefings

6:00 Dramatic Reading Contest Begins

6:50 Break

7:00 International Speech Contest Begins

7:50 Announcements

7:55 Awards Ceremony

8:00 Everybody Goes Home!

6 contestants 5–7 min, ea. 1 min for judges between contestants.

5 min to award all trophies.

No acceptance speeches!

Contest Officials

Toastmaster—Valiant S. Vetter, CTM

Chief Judge—Jyothi SanJuan, CTM

Timers—Dolores Gordon, CTM

& Cathy Jackson

Very professional!

Ballot Counters—John Barry, CTM,

Michaline Jekot, DTM, James Sienzant, ATM

Sgt. at Arms—John F. Barry, CTM

Where Do You See Yourself in the World of Six-Minute Speeches <u>and</u> Electronic Presentations?

The world of speakers is changing dramatically.

This book concerns itself with one of the *two* major changes that are happening wherever people are communicating with audiences.

■ The speakers are talking shorter. Not all of them, as we shall soon see, but it is a definite and important trend.

■ The second major development is the increasing use of computer-based presentation systems that rely upon software to produce brilliant multimedia effects.

When these two developments come together, an interesting question arises. *What happens to the speaker?*

In most cases, adjustments must be made.

Not only will the speaker have to adjust to *less time* in the spotlight—the speaker will have to *share* the spotlight with the computer's visual impact.

Eventually, you're going to have to ask yourself, "What kind of a speaker do I want to be?"

You've got four choices. None of them are dreadful—and you can be effective in any of them.

The Speaker Is All!

You've seen this speaker dozens of times—and he or she isn't likely to go away no matter how sophisticated the electronic equipment becomes.

- Has the instincts of an orator. Is usually paid a hefty fee. The audience expects "a show"—so time isn't a critical factor.

- Speaks directly to the audience. Uses few, if any, visual aids. Doesn't use *anything* that might detract from the speaker's "star quality." However, some "stars" are now speaking to remote audiences via live video.

- Has a reputation. Could be a national hero. Or a politician. Or an evangelist. Think of motivational speaker Zig Ziglar as a prime example of "The Speaker Is All."

The Speaker Dominates

This is an effective speaking arrangement for a certain kind of executive. It provides total control of a meeting *through* an audio/visual master control panel. This touch panel is always in the same place and always identifies who's running the meeting. The executive seated at the "black box" determines who speaks, for how long, and what graphics are shown. It is a *command post*.

■ Since the speaker has control of the meeting in an absolute sense, he or she can allot times and call on people by merely dominating the multimedia display.

■ If you choose to become this type of speaker, you must know how to handle the equipment, almost like an orchestra conductor. This is a speaking style for anyone who likes the idea of running the show, and showing who's boss.

The Reluctant Dragon

This speaker isn't crazy about speaking engagements. See him peeking out from behind that vertical screen? He'll probably stay right there until the end, then come forward and say a few words. Articulate and gracious, but reluctant.

■   This speaker likes the new software as a presentation aid mainly because it takes the pressure off of her or him. For a big sales meeting, the CEO can make a modest appearance and yet look pretty spectacular with a little audio/visual assistance. Many CEOs, men and women, fit into this group.

■   If you like the idea of letting your electronics do the "performing," this could be the category for you.

The Software as Speaker

Now, we are moving so far into the future that you won't see many representatives of this category.

- The software makes the presentation and the speaker stands by—maybe for Q & A afterward.

- The software is precisely timed, probably around six minutes—maybe a bit longer.

- With the software serving as speaker, conventions will become much more theaterlike. Interaction between the audience and the electronic equipment could become intense.

- The speaker becomes a "monitor"—watching from the wings—gauging response, perhaps changing the content electronically to fit the mood of the audience.

This is where the future is headed. Maybe it's not for you. Maybe you don't want to share the stage with *anything*. Okay. We will always have speakers who love the limelight. Maybe you'd rather dominate the software but still use it to suit your proposes. Okay. Or maybe you're a "reluctant dragon." That's okay, too.

Interact with this section and project yourself *as a speaker* into the future. Where do you see yourself?

SHORT TAKES

I don't care how much
a man talks if he only says it
in a few words
—Josh Billings
American Humorist

The longer the selling process,
the less likely the close.
—Dr. Forbes Ley,
The Best Seller

PART FOUR

Cutting Costs and Solving Problems in Six Minutes

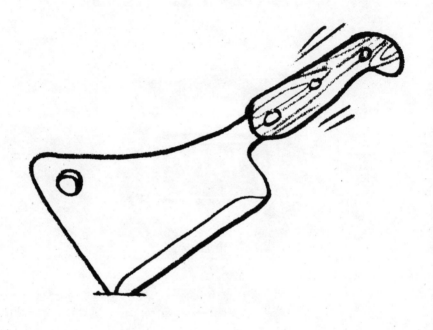

CHAPTER 13

Cutting Costs with a **Cleaver**

Six "Radical Ideas" That Can Slash Your Meeting Costs

With all of those new words floating around—reengineering, restructuring, reinventing, downsizing, dejobbing, devolution, delayering, and streamlining—I've never heard a one of them applied to the common, old everyday meeting.

Has anybody in your company ever said, "Let's get together this afternoon and reengineer our meeting structure?"

Meetings seem to get a free ride. People come late, glaze over, daydream, lose track of time, and the costs just float right out the window.

Enough already! The six "radical ideas" on the next page attempt to introduce cost control to the meeting room. They don't try to reinvent anything—or delayer it—they just strive to bring a little efficiency to it.

Take a look. Are the ideas really "radical"? Or just overdue?

IMPORTANT NOTICE

(To be sent to all employees who call
or attend meetings)

Idea #1: Before you call a meeting, ask yourself this question: What is the Burning Issue here? If there is no Burning Issue, resolve the matter by fax or conference call. *NOTE: This means we aren't going to have any more weekly meetings, or monthly meetings, or even annual meetings.*

Idea #2: In our internal meetings, no one speaks for over six minutes. If you can't tell us what we need to know in six minutes, write a report and distribute it. Make sure the detail of the report is preceded by an executive summary.

Idea #3: Feel free to walk out of any presentation that has been poorly prepared and is wasting your time.

Idea #4: We have no need for people to "front" the work of others. The person who created the work will take full responsibility for it—including whatever explanation is needed.

Idea #5: No meeting in this company will start without an agenda that has been sent to all attendees at least 24 hours before the meeting.

Idea #6: Minutes will be distributed within one hour after every meeting. Who was there, what was decided, next steps —including who is responsible for which tasks. Deadlines will be set.

CALLER OF THE MEETING

AGENDA

Date and time of meeting:

Subject of meeting:

Issues to be resolved:

Those attending:

Special assignments for meeting:
(speakers, subjects—six minutes each)

Meeting will be over at:

(caller of meeting)

SHORT TAKES

Perhaps hell is nothing more
than an enormous conference
of those who, with little
or nothing to say,
take an eternity to say it.

—Dudley C. Stone,
executive, Journal of
Systems Management

"THY SERMON RUNNETH OVER."

*S*ix "Little Ideas" That Can Cut Your Meeting Costs Even More

This is a book on a simple mission: It asks you to help yourself. Namely, cut your speakers down to six minutes and see what happens to your productivity.

We offered some "radical ideas" to get you started in the preceding pages. Now, here are some more "specifics"—not as demanding this time—on how to cut still more costs out of your meetings.

Did you know, for instance, that big corporations can squander as much as a million dollars a year by *not starting meetings on time*?

Maybe the people simply don't show up, or maybe they're kidding around. Either way, nothing happens for the first ten minutes. Multiply that ten-minute lag—which eventually becomes a corporate habit—by the number of people who go to meetings in any one company, and you've got yourself a major waste of money that isn't going to show up on anybody's balance sheet.

Here are some "little things" that can save you a lot of money you may not know you're wasting:

1. **Try any four of these meeting starters at your next meeting. Results guaranteed!**
   - Actually start on time. This should have a lasting "shock value."
   - Flick the lights throughout your office space.
   - Let your in-house comic get on the intercom and improvise an announcement about the meeting getting under way and what will happen to latecomers.
   - Let your treasurer get on the intercom and announce that everybody who is late to the meeting will be fined. (This idea came from Congress, of all places.)
   - Hire a CEO who gets hysterical about starting meetings on time and carries a little black book to note the late arrivals.
   - Dole out espresso and blueberry muffins to everybody who arrives ahead of time. Cut off the supply to all latecomers (sounds a bit draconian, but it works.)

2. **Draw a picture of what's going to happen.** The four squares below, with their little jotty notes, could be time-saving graphics in your next meeting. Draw everything—just as indicated below—on some big squares of paper at the start of your meeting. Tack the squares to the wall, side by side, and leave them up there in full view until the meeting is over. The purpose here is blessedly simple: "Nobody is going to forget anything about this meeting—including the time it's supposed to be over—because everything is up there on the wall where you can't possibly miss it." You'll have to fill in the four lines under the squares according to your plans for the meeting. P.S.: Feel free to make the letters in the squares different colors—or whatever artistic touches you want to add.

You'll be amazed by the way this graphic keeps people alert and involved throughout the meeting. They've got no excuses to daydream. They know *why* the meeting was called; *how* it will be managed; *when* it will be over; and *what* everybody's supposed to do. Let's call this idea an ACTion device for shortening lengthy meetings.

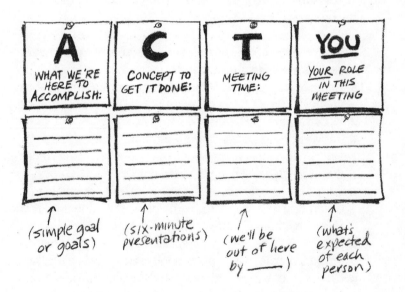

3. **Appoint a tough "judge" from the group of people who will attend.** He or she should know meeting rooms like experienced judges know courtrooms. Maybe this person is a "facilitator" you've brought in from outside—or maybe it's someone who can really run a meeting and would have been a member of the group anyway. This is someone who can call "time" on meeting monopolists (every organization has at least one). Like a real judge, a meeting judge can rule on what's relevant and what's not. He or she can set time limits on everybody (like six minutes or less). And your judge should be someone who has stored up enough respect from the group that everybody can walk out of the meeting "still friends."

Idea for the judge: Put one of those kitchen timers in the middle of the conference table. Set it for six minutes just before the speaker starts. It will make little clicking sounds as time passes. Make sure it's facing the speaker when the sixth minute begins.

4. **The more people you invite to your meeting, the longer your meeting will be.** This is a law of meeting logistics that you can count on when all else fails. In a big meeting, everybody has to show off a little. Everybody has to say something, just to have something on the record—to prove he or she was thinking and not dozing off. (Consultants *urge* their clients to never leave a meeting without opening their mouths.) The reverse of this law is equally true. The fewer people you invite, the shorter your meeting will be.

5. **What you've learned in leaving voice-mail messages could help you shorten person-to-person meetings.** This is a very short story.

My mother was talking on the phone. Here's the way it went:

"Hi, Linda! This is your grandmother. I understand you're looking for a slide projector—to practice your speech. I have one you can use. Just call back and say 'yes' or 'no.' If you want it, I'll leave it on the back porch tonight and you can pick it up in the morning. Bye!"

133

I walked into the room where my mother had just hung up. "My gosh, Mother," I said, "that was the most concise conversation you have ever had."

My mother looked at me and said, "Oh . . . Linda wasn't there. I'm just learning how to use voice mail."

There's an insight in there somewhere. People can be concise when the circumstances dictate conciseness. Apply a little voice-mail technique in your next meeting and see what happens.

6. **Quick tips for furnishing the meeting room that will reduce the time it's used.**

- Install a clock on the wall where the presenter can see it without having to put on his or her glasses.
- Make the seats just a tiny bit uncomfortable. They should be firm, upright, businesslike. If they could talk, they would say, "Don't lean back. Don't slump over. Don't get too comfortable. This is a meeting, damn it!" Big, puffy, marshmallow seats can totally diffuse the dynamic tension that every good meeting should have.
- Post a sign outside the door. "Meeting in Progress. Do Not Enter."
- Take all of the seats out of the conference room and invite attendees to stroll about, studying and discussing exhibits on the walls. Open Market, a business consultant and maker of software for the Internet, uses this technique to cut meeting time (and windy speeches).
- Remove the telephone. Leave word that only emergency calls will be taken. (Have you ever noticed how one phone call can drive a meeting *nuts*? Everybody ignores the speaker and leans toward the phone. "Is it for me? Is it for me?")
- Check the ventilation. Nothing puts a meeting on the nod as fast as a rickety ventilating system. To keep the brain moving, keep the air moving.

SHORT TAKES

Congress is so strange.
A man gets up to speak.
Nobody listens—
then everybody disagrees.

—A Russian observer
of the U.S. Congress

Let's hear it for the speaker
who hops to the platform,
skips his introduction, and
jumps to his conclusion.

—Wall Street Journal

An abundance of words
often conceals a lack of ideas.

—Hippias of Elias,
Greek scholar,
approx. 500 B.C.

"**W**here's The Payoff?"

At one time, Arthur Clark was the CEO of a worldwide integrated marketing company. He enjoyed "the game of business" and was always at least 10 steps ahead of everybody in the room. He was also the toughest boss I've ever had.

Now, he has retired from the marketing company and started up his own entrepreneurial business. In the process, he has mellowed out.

Shortly before this book went to press, I was sitting in his office. He was leaning back in his Eames chair, hands clasped behind his head, feet propped on his desk—with Chicago sprawled out behind him.

"Well," he said, "I read your manuscript like you told me to." There was a pause. "You know me," he said, **"I'm an old hound dog about payoffs. How do I know your idea is going to work for *me*?"**

I started thumbing through the pages of the manuscript.

"Look, before you get all defensive, let's just talk about it," he said.

He loved the *exploration* of business, especially costs.

"How many conference rooms did we have when you and I were working together?"

"Four," I said. "One on each floor. The idea was to have one conference room per department."

"Yeah, that was my idea. I thought by keeping the number of conference rooms small, we'd have fewer meetings."

"Did it work?"

"No," he replied, "but it really kept the conference rooms booked up."

"And I remember quite a few meetings in *your* office. In fact, I'll never forget them."

He chose to ignore my recollection.

"Let's say the conference rooms were busy 75 percent of the time, and I was at least partly successful in holding the costs down by keeping the meetings small . . . seldom more than four people per meeting.

"Okay, Arthur, but five is probably closer to reality."

"Let's compromise on *four.*"

"Fine."

"During an eight-hour day, the conference rooms were occupied for at least six hours, I'd say. I know because my secretary booked the rooms. How *long* were the meetings? Got any idea?"

"The national average is an hour and a half."

"Our meetings weren't that long," he said. "Our meetings were more like an hour."

"All right."

Suddenly, he was sitting up straight, drilling numbers into his calculator.

"If the average salary of the people attending the meeting was $55,000 a year—actually, that's low for these days. Let's say $65,000 for right now—then four people attending a one-hour meeting costs $130 an hour—$32.50 a person." His calculator clicked to a stop.

"All right," I said, anxious to get into it with him, "but *that's pure meeting time.*"

"What does that mean?" he asked.

"Well, according to the experts, you have to take the base pay of those attending the meetings and *double* it—because every meeting requires a certain amount of reading, reviewing, researching—you know all the stuff that goes into meetings."

"Mostly politics," he said.

"But it takes time."

"All right."

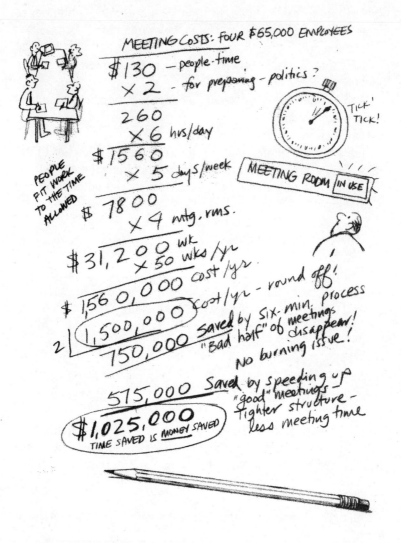

MEETING COSTS: FOUR $65,000 EMPLOYEES

$130 — people-time
× 2 - for preparing - politics?
260
× 6 hrs/day
$1560
× 5 days/week   MEETING ROOM IN USE
$7800
× 4 mtg. rms.
$31,200 wk
× 50 wks/yr
$1,560,000 cost/yr.
2 | $1,500,000 cost/yr - round off!
750,000 saved by six-min. process
"Bad half" of meetings disappear!
No burning issue!
575,000 saved by speeding up
"good" meetings —
tighter structure —
less meeting time
$1,025,000
TIME SAVED IS MONEY SAVED

PEOPLE FIT WORK TO THE TIME ALLOWED

TICK TICK!

"So, at $260 an hour, that's $1,560 a day, or $7,800 a week." I did the arithmetic this time.

"You forgot the *four* conference rooms." Arthur poked a number into his calculator. "You're up to $31,200 a week—or over a million five a year—just for meetings." He was impressed. "How much of that could be saved by your six-minute plan?"

"Well, executives seem to agree that *half* of all meetings are an utter and absolute waste of time. They get very vocal about it. And the research backs them up. A recent survey pegged 'the waste factor' of the 33 million business meetings held in America every business day at 49 percent."

"I'm not surprised, but it is pretty damn shocking."

"Ever heard of Mark McCormack?"

"Sure—the sports agent."

"Right. He spends most of his life in meetings—and he says that half of the scheduled meetings in the average American company could be done away with and never be missed."

"How do I know which half to drop?"

"You don't. You just apply the ideas in the book. The tight agenda, the prompt starting time, the strict adherence to the six-minute presentation, the focused interaction, and then you tell everybody that a decision should be reached in 25 minutes—half an hour, total."

"How do I know it will work?"

"I never thought I'd get that question from you, Arthur."

"Why not?"

"Because you taught me the answer." He waited for the answer.

"People always fit the work into the time allowed. Whatever time you give 'em to do a job, they'll fill it."

Arthur was pleased. "You're right. It never fails. That's how every advance in business history has been made. Somebody told somebody it had to be done faster."

"Somebody like you, Arthur."

"Well, deadlines do motivate."

"And if you don't get a decision within the deadline, you can safely assume that there wasn't any Burning Issue to begin with."

"The bad meetings just disappear?"

"No question. The bad half of your meetings will weed itself out as soon as you apply the six-minute limit. That's because the boiling down of the issue to six minutes will reveal that there is no issue to have a meeting about."

"Great. We've saved $750,000 of the million five right there. What about the strong half?"

"The strong half gets stronger when the process is condensed—it never fails. Meanwhile, you pick up $375,000 in saved time."

"So, half of the meetings just go away and the other half are half as long—is that it?"

"You got it—and you've saved well over a million dollars in time, plus you've got yourself a much more productive organization."

"Sounds better when we talk it through," he said.

"Which reminds me," I said, trying not to sound like a wise guy. "We didn't include the meetings in your office."

"Oh those were different—I ran them. They were *very* efficient."

He smiled, but I couldn't tell if he was joking or just pleased with himself. I decided not to push it.

GUT CHECK:
Start here to figure *your* meeting costs

Average Annual Salary:	Hourly Cost of Meeting:					
$100,000	$200	$400	$600	$800	$1,000	$2,000
$75,000	$150	$300	$450	$600	$750	$1,500
$62,500	$125	$250	$375	$500	$625	$1,250
$50,000	$100	$200	$300	$400	$500	$1,000
$37,500	$75	$150	$225	$300	$375	$750
$25,000	$50	$100	$150	$200	$250	$500
	2	4	6	8	10	20

Number of attendees

Chart reprinted with permission from *Mastering Meetings: Discovering the Hidden Potential of Effective Business Meetings,* by the 3M Meeting Management Team with Jeanine Drew (McGraw-Hill, 1994).

Next meeting you're in, use this little chart to noodle out your costs by the hour, by the week, even by the year. The results may spur you to Say It in Six.

CHAPTER 14

Personal Payoffs of the Six-Minute System, Including One That Could **Save Your Job**

*T*he Case of the Crooked Pole

Everybody's afraid of being hauled into traffic court. If you live in Chicago, you have good reason.

The traffic court on North LaSalle in downtown Chicago is an industry unto itself. As you approach the building, it looks like a cross between the old Chicago Stadium and the Cook County Jail. Parking lots beckon from every side, offering lots of space—starting at $8.25 for the first hour.

The first floor is teeming with people, all looking like they wished they were somewhere else. Long lines extend back from windows offering everything from "boot hearings" to "payments." Nothing sounds like something you'd want to do.

I was there as a witness. My fiancée, Peggy, was there as a defendant, *unjustly accused* (I had been instructed to add). I was also there to coach a six-minute speech which was to be delivered by the defendant herself in Hearing Room 2 to Mr. David B. Atkins, hearing officer.

As we waited in one of the dozens of lines, the defendant was nervous. "It's just a matter of principle," she kept saying. Her car had been ticketed one lazy Sunday afternoon and hauled off to the pound. Thinking it had been stolen, she called the police—only to find that they had it. At that point, it was clearly more than a matter of principle. She was mad.

Meanwhile, as we sat waiting on the back bench of Hearing Room 2, I was quietly coaching her. "Don't forget to say 'good morning,' that's very important. Also, state the Burning Issue right off the bat. Have you got your evidence?"

"Yes, yes," she said. "Why don't you just concentrate on what *you're* going to say?"

What a team, I thought.

"Next," the hearing officer said in an airline captain's tone. We marched up to the platform where Mr. Atkins was sitting.

"Good morning," my fiancée said in a loud, clear voice.

The hearing officer never looked up from his computer. My fiancée handed over the pile of paperwork that had accumulated over the $25 fine and $150 towing charge.

"Start fast, start fast," I was thinking.

"The issue is this," my fiancée said, as if reading my mind. "The issue is whether my car was parked in a bus loading zone or not."

Mr. Atkins looked up from his computer for the first time. I had the feeling he had never heard such an assertive beginning.

"Yes, go on."

"I believe that the reason I was given a ticket by the police officer was that he thought I was parked in the bus loading zone."

Mr. Atkins nodded.

"But," my fiancée added quickly, "there was no way the officer could have been sure of that because one of the signs—identifying the south end of the zone—was gone. Only the pole was there—and it was crooked, like someone had hit it. Here. Let me show you this photograph of the scene."

She whipped out her snapshots. Mr. Atkins leaned forward. There was the pole, all right. No sign. Crooked, too.

"This pole," she pointed it out on the snapshot, "*might* have been the south end of the bus zone, but how was anyone to know?"

The hearing officer looked back at her.

"You see," she continued, "there was no yellow line on the curbing where I was parked. And my car—indicated by the X—was over 89 feet away from the north end of the bus stop."

She then produced her *pièce de résistance*. Her map—with all measurements clearly shown. "Here is my car," she said, pointing to the X, "23 feet from the bus stop pavement—right between the snow sign and the crooked pole which has no sign."

Make your case with snapshots (the idea made tangible).

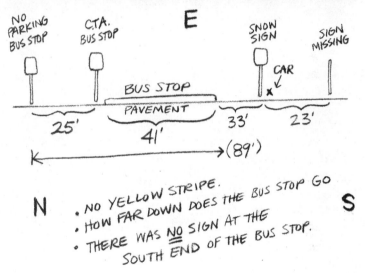

The map was an audio/visual showstopper. It was almost like a scene from *Matlock*.

The hearing officer stared at the map. She had also written the three main points in her argument just below the map. Perfect!

David B. Atkins, hearing officer of Hearing Room 2—Chicago Traffic Court Building—was impressed.

"Well, I see what you mean."

"Thank you, sir, I've really worked on this. It's a matter of principle."

"I see that," Mr. Atkins said.

He gave his computer one final glance.

"Since you have no previous record—and you have raised a defense sufficient to rebut the prima facie case—I'm going to hold that you are not liable."

My fiancée looked like she had just won a landmark case in the Supreme Court.

"Oh, thank you, your honor."

"Just take these papers to one of the windows outside."

As we inched slowly forward in line, I thought, "What a perfect place for a six-minute speech." Actually, it took us about four minutes—not counting the time in line.

```
I, DAVID B. ATKINS, A DULY APPOINTED HEARING OFFICER,
FIND THAT THE NOTICE OF PARKING VIOLATION ESTABLISHES
A PRIMA FACIE CASE.  RESPONDENT HAS RAISED A DEFENSE
UNDER SECTION 9-100-060 (5) WHICH IS SUFFICIENT TO
REBUT THE PRIMA FACIE CASE.  THE RESPONDENT NAMED
ABOVE IS NOT LIABLE.

NO FURTHER ACTION IS REQUIRED.
```

Saving You from Downsizing

Fortune magazine has called it "ceaseless reorganization."

For the average longtime worker in American industry, "ceaseless reorganization" has been like an earthquake rumbling under his or her work station.

Jobs vanish. One employee showed up with his daughter on "Take Your Daughter to Work Day" and was told that his job had been reorganized right out of existence. It was a long ride home.

The most vulnerable employees in U.S. industry are those who are regarded as little more than numbers. Their files are spotless, but also empty.

For those people, the only hope is to get their stories into circulation, so that—eventually—they will show up in a database somewhere as being workers who are uniquely qualified and exceptionally capable.

This chapter provides you an interactive exercise that may help you get your name and your qualifications into circulation where they will do you the most good.

Let's Just Say . . .

Let's just say that you worked for one of those companies that is always trying to save money.

Let's just say that the time-study experts have been snooping around your workstation.

Let's just say that your boss has asked you to tell him or her why you should be retained while other people are being let go.

Let's just say you were asked to state your own best case in six minutes or less.

Could you do it?

If You Said . . .

If you said, "Gee, I don't know," how can you expect your boss to speak up for you—strongly and succinctly—if you're not sure you could do it yourself?

Never fear. Help is here—in an interactive exercise that could help you save your job.

How to State Your Case

1. The Burning Issue:

Why should we keep you and fire others?

_____

_____

_____

_____

_____

II. Overview:

What is your overall impact upon the company?

_____

_____

_____

_____

_____

_____

III. What makes you worth more?

What **IDEAS** have you had lately?_____

_____

_____

_____

_____

IV. The Payoff: What's your candid assessment of

your day-to-day performance? _____

_____

_____

_____

_____

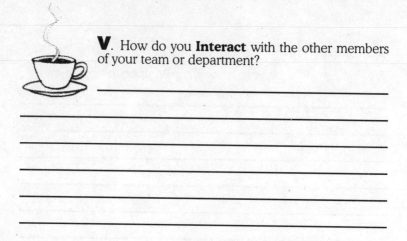

V. How do you **Interact** with the other members of your team or department?

_____

_____

_____

_____

_____

_____

The exercise above comes right out of the
six-minute structure. If you put your answers
together, what kind of case would they make?

Does This Sound Like You?

Try saying your answers out loud.

I.   There's a Burning Issue Here. Who can deliver more value for the dollar? I can name you three separate projects where my ideas have saved the company money.

II.   What Do I Do That's Different? I really study the projects I'm assigned to. Ask the team leaders. I see things from *inside* my assignment, and I see things from *outside*. I make sure I understand the project strategy, the team strategy, and the strategy of my own assignment. Nobody else does that.

III.   Ideas? Sure! I suggested that every member of the team should be able to do somebody else's job. Not just as a fill-in. Really do it. This gives us all kinds of flexibility. I'm the one who suggested that the same team shouldn't be put together more than once—that every project deserved at least two people who haven't worked together before. Change is good for teams. It keeps them fresh. I'm always thinking who I'd like to work with on my next team—who I'll learn from—and who I can help. I try to stay ahead of the game—and it pays off for the company.

IV.   Day to Day, I'm always here. I haven't missed a day since I started. I don't cost money, I save money. I look for potential "glitches" on every project. I don't leave loose ends for somebody else to clean up. There are never any surprises when the bills come in. Nobody has to worry about my role in the project. Ask my team leaders. I take my job seriously.

V.   With My Fellow Employees, I help where I can—I'm not pushy. With today's teams, you've got to be sensitive to where the other people are coming from. I take pride in the way I handle myself inside the team. I know how to make an extra contribution to the company without upsetting the teamwork that we try so hard to maintain around here. I really work at it. You've got to be understanding with others, but you've got to be competitive in our own performance. That's a delicate balance. I can handle it.

Does that sound like you? If it doesn't, what do *you* sound like?

Just fill in the lines starting on page 146. Once you've stated your case for yourself, you'll find that it becomes much easier to state your case to others—including your boss. And, these days, you never know when you might need a good, strong voice on your behalf.

SHORT TAKE

Hi! I'm in a meeting now, but your message is very important to me. . . .

—Voice mail of a person who attends too many meetings

EPILOGUE

What's the Payoff
for **You?**

When you sit down after making your first six-minute talk, what have you said about yourself?

■ You've shown your audience that you've *listened*. They've been saying it for years—they are fed to the teeth with long, dreary speeches. That's what most of the quotes in this book—from Mark Twain to Uncle Vanya—have been saying in their own winsome ways.

■ You've demonstrated that you're a risk-taker in a field of behavior that is not known for risk taking.

■ You've put forth an effective effort to save your audience precious *time*. You've done a lot of work to compress a great deal of information into a form that is easy to grasp and lasts only six minutes. You've shown that you are willing to *step up* and extend yourself for the good of the team.

■ You've cleared the way for a *decision* to be made. You've increased the likelihood that it will be the *right* decision.

■ You've laid it on the line. Six minutes requires that you say *exactly* what you mean. You've been absolutely honest with your family, your team at work, your church group, or whoever you've been talking to.

Sounds like your first six-minute speech has said some impressive things about *you*. *Congratulations!* I wish you nothing but the best in a world of less talk, more meaning, and no baloney.

Ron Hoff

SHORT TAKE

We all want to talk.
We've done nothing but talk
for fifty years.
And now I say enough!
—Dialogue from Vanya on
42nd Street, *a film adaptation
by David Mamet of
Chekhov's Uncle Vanya*

Extra Worksheets have been included on
the following pages. Use them to *Say It in
Six*. And let met know how everything
goes. Does brevity work for you? How do
your audiences feel about it? Any comments, bouquets, or brickbats? It's interaction time!

Ron Hoff
c/o Andrews and McMeel
4520 Main Street
Kansas City, MO 64111

"SAY IT IN SIX" STEP-BY-STEP WORKSHEET

1 *"Let's get right to the point. There's a **burning issue** here that we need to discuss."* _____

_____

_____

_____

_____

_____

_____

2 *"Here's a quick **overview**—just a bit of background."*

_____

_____

_____

_____

_____

3 *"This led to an **idea**. . . ."* _____

_____

_____

_____

_____

_____

_____

_____

_____

_____

_____

4 *"The idea will more than pay for itself. Here's the* **payoff**. . . ." _____

_____

_____

_____

_____

_____

5 *"Here's* **what we need** *from you to get going. . . ."*

_____

_____

_____

_____

_____

_____

"SAY IT IN SIX" STEP-BY-STEP WORKSHEET

1 *"Let's get right to the point. There's a **burning issue** here that we need to discuss."* _____ .

_____

_____

_____

_____

_____

_____

2 *"Here's a quick **overview**—just a bit of background."*

_____

_____

_____

_____

_____

3 *"This led to an **idea**. . . ."* _____

_____

_____

_____

_____

_____

_____

_____

_____

_____

4 *"The idea will more than pay for itself. Here's the* **payoff**. . . ."_____

_____

_____

_____

_____

5 *"Here's* **what we need** *from you to get going. . . ."*

_____

_____

_____

_____

_____

"SAY IT IN SIX" STEP-BY-STEP WORKSHEET

1 *"Let's get right to the point. There's a **burning issue** here that we need to discuss."* _____

_____

_____

_____

_____

_____

_____

2 *"Here's a quick **overview**—just a bit of background."*

_____

_____

_____

_____

_____

3 *"This led to an **idea**. . . ."* _____

_____

_____

_____

_____

4 *"The idea will more than pay for itself. Here's the* **payoff**. . . ." _____

_____

_____

_____

_____

_____

5 *"Here's* **what we need** *from you to get going. . . ."*

_____

_____

_____

_____

_____

About the Author

Ron Hoff is one of America's leading speakers and presentation coaches. As an executive in the major leagues of marketing and advertising, he has made literally hundreds of multi-million-dollar presentations. His first book, *"I Can See You Naked": A Fearless Guide to Making Great Presentations,* was selected by 16 book clubs and translated into Russian and Chinese. His byline has appeared in the *New York Times, Wall Street Journal, Chicago Tribune,* and other publications. He is a frequent keynote speaker.